That's
Life

©2022 by Barbara L. Sellers

All rights reserved. No part of this publication may be reproduced or transmitted in any form or by any means, electronic or mechanical, including photocopying, recording, or any other information storage and retrieval system, without the written permission of the author or publisher.

Internet addresses given in this book were accurate at the time it went to press.

Printed in the United States of America

Published in Hellertown, PA

Cover and interior design and illustrations by

Library of Congress 2022911618

ISBN: 978-1-958711-01-9

2 4 6 8 10 9 7 5 3 1

For more information or to place bulk orders, contact the publisher at Jennifer@BrightCommunications.net.

Bright
COMMUNICATIONS

BrightCommunications.net

To four people who encouraged me to pursue and excel in my professional writing career: my grandmother Marian Harrison Brewster, my seventh-grade English teacher Betty Bradfield, my senior English teacher Ordell (Lee) Paulson, and former Chief of Army Newspapers Sergeant Major Gary G. Beylickjian

CONTENTS

PREFACE

"IF YOU EVER have a motorcycle accident, you will find out that the human head is not a big, rubber ball after all. Upon impact, it's more like a ripe melon."

I ended my story with these two lines when I wrote about how important it is for all motorcycle riders to always wear approved safety helmets. I never kept a copy of that story, but my university professor raved about my powerful ending. She said I left my readers with a vivid image of what happens when a ripe melon is dropped onto a hard surface, and it literally gave her goose bumps. Now I wish I had kept a copy of that story because it might have saved lives. In fact, my first husband ended up in a hospital bed instead of the morgue because I insisted that he buy a safety helmet eight hours before he went motorcycle riding with a few of his more-experienced biker friends.

If we are lucky enough to live to be a ripe old age, most of us have several stories locked inside our memory banks. Many of our stories should be told and shared with others, but never are. By sharing our life experiences and stories, we can learn valuable lessons from each other. When it was more common for parents and/or grandparents to live with their adult children or grandchildren, young family members grew up hearing about their family history. They got a much stronger sense of family roots, and they also got a much stronger sense of patriotism and love of our country, too, when they heard how uncles or grandparents fought for our freedom in previous wars. That seldom happens anymore.

That's one reason why I'm writing this book: to preserve some of my stories for future generations of family members and other readers who are growing up in a much different time.

Poetry can be very subjective, but I hope my readers will enjoy my poems. Nine out of 10 of my short stories are true, but some of them carry valuable lessons, too. At least one of my stories involves some of my sisters and brothers. For consistency with my first book, *Get Tough or Die: Why I Forgave My Parents for My Abusive Childhood*, I am using the same first names in this book and no last names are used.

"No matter who you meet in life, you take something from them, positive or negative," Gary Allen said. Throughout our lives, the people we come in contact with are usually left better or worse off for having known us. The kind of people we include in our lives often determines who and what we become, and that's why inspirational speakers often encourage us to surround ourselves with people who lift us up and let go of those who put us down. That does not mean, however, that we should let go of everyone who disagrees with us. Of course, constant disagreements are never good, but some friendly disagreements are actually healthy. Often the people who have the courage to disagree with us end up helping us the most. We need to have some people in our lives with different viewpoints to help us maintain an open mind, gain new perspectives, and become the best that we can be.

I hope you enjoy reading my poetry and short stories. You can also follow me on my "Get Tough or Die" Facebook Page or at BarbaraSellers.com.

PART I

Poetry

My first marriage to the late Franklin R. Harvey.

Love Poems

My second marriage to (Ret.) Lt. Col. Donald R. Sellers.

THE YOU I LOVED

Dedicated to my late first husband

Where is the YOU who was loyal and caring?
And where is the love we started out sharing?

The YOU I remember was steadfast and true.
Whatever happened to that kind of YOU?

I love the YOU that YOU used to be.
That part of YOU was a good part of me.

But the new kind of YOU that YOU have become
That is the YOU I'm now turning from.

Still, I miss YOU, the YOU that I know,
The YOU that I love. Where did YOU go?

THE CHEATING GAME

When lovers start the cheating game, they call it by another name.
Perhaps at first, they're only friends, but that's not how it
    usually ends.
When guilt sets in, they soon discover their "pretend friend"
    is their lover.
What started out as harmless fun could end up hurting everyone.

Things never do look quite the same when addressed by the
    right name.
If it's ok, you'll tell the truth, and if you can't, it's solid proof
You better make a quick retraction before you carry out the action.
But call it something sweet and boast, you'll be the one
    deceived the most.

If you don't like this losing game, you only have yourself to blame.
So, learn to live in constant fear that your loving spouse will hear
About the lies told to conceal everything you didn't reveal.
Then be prepared to say goodbye when it's too late to explain why.

And so, before you play this game, you better call it by its name.
And read the first important rule: Each player has to be a fool.
Such warnings should give you a scare but go ahead if you don't care.
Chances are once done and said, you'll wish you stayed at home instead.

THE PLANTS YOU GAVE ME

Dedicated to the late Russell Jones

The plants that you gave me had a story to tell,
For the way that they grew explains it so well.
My first plant was little, but I liked it a lot.
The buds promised flowers like the love that we sought.

Though I cared for the plants just as well as I could,
Perhaps they didn't have all the sunshine they should.
The big, rubber tree looked so healthy and strong.
I thought, like our love, it would last very long.

But the rubber tree withered, and one day it died,
And soon after that, my broken heart cried.
Only one plant remains that I cannot touch,
'Cause needles of cactus hurt me too much.

Yet, a flowering cactus is an unusual kind.
Like the memory of love that you left behind.

I KNEW HIM

Oh, I knew him ...
At least I knew him
An ordinary way.
Then I saw him ...
I really saw him
For the first time today,
Beneath his smile.
He often smiled
But never quite so bright.
I just liked him.
I always liked him,
But I'm in love tonight.

TRUE LOVE

So many times, I wondered why
If it was love, how did it die?
It seemed like love. It filled a need.
But true love grows just like a seed.

True love is not a simple thing,
Three tender words and diamond ring.
True love can't hurt or lie or cheat.
That is not love: It's called deceit.

True love is love without demands
Of perfection. It understands
And freely gives to someone else
Everything you want yourself.

True love is more than I can say,
But it can't last when it's one way.
True love is strong. It would endure.
So, was it love? I'm NOT too sure.

ALONE

She looks out beyond the sand
Just as two lovers kiss.
Then turns her head to when she wed
And knew the lover's bliss.

On the beach alone and cold,
She thinks of times gone by.
A teardrop falls as she recalls
How such a love can die.

If they knew a love so true
Could end just like a dance,
If they were me, if they could see,
Would they still take a chance?

SOMETIMES

Sometimes when I see you
I feel a sense of family again.
And a happy memory of past togetherness
Wants to make my heart smile.
And sometimes, just sometimes,
I almost say, "I need you!"
But my hurt part won't let me,
And your guilt part won't listen.
So, I hide the love sign ...
Tuck it neatly in a file,
Where I'll keep it for a while,
Just collecting dust.
Not because I want to, but my ego says I must.
And sometimes, still sometimes,
I feel angry and betrayed
'Cause the promises we made were broken.
And no matter what the reason,
It feels worse than treason.
But in cheating lovers' war games
There are no white peace flags,
No rejoicing and no winners.
Only victims of a time bomb
Controlled by human sinners.

ROMANTIC LOVE

Looking for love
Two silhouettes together
Hand in hand.
On the deserted beach
They discover
The pleasure of living.

Falling in love
Two lovers in the sunset
Face to face.
Beyond the ocean waves
They explore
The limits of giving.

Sharing pure love
A man and a woman united
Soul to soul.
Under the dim moonlight
They devour
The passion of loving.

ONE-NIGHT STAND

Went to a dance, loud music played.
Stared in a trance while bodies swayed.
What do they want? Why are they here?
Some of them drown themselves in beer.

I hear them laugh and see them flirt,
But underneath I know they hurt.
They have no names, just shape and size.
They act sincere, while living lies.

Without meaning, like mating birds.
No emotions, just empty words.
So, they perform from near and far
And no one asks them who they are.

WOUNDED LOVERS

Two lonely, wounded lovers
Just one day chanced to meet.
They could be very happy
But their wounds are very deep.

Two leery, wounded lovers
Will their past wounds ever heal
Enough to take a chance again
And know their love is real?

BROWN EYES

Dedicated to Bill W.

Trusting brown eyes
Committed his love
For seventeen years.
Now silently suffer
And cry without tears.

Foolish brown eyes
Rejecting the truth
That her love is gone,
Still privately singing
A miracle song.

Lonely brown eyes,
Magnetic brown eyes,
Will they ever see
The blue eyes of love
That are yearning in me?

YESTERDAY MOMENTS

All yesterday moments
Cannot be erased.
For sooner or later
They have to be faced.

Our yesterday laughter,
Our yesterday schemes,
Our yesterday feelings,
Our yesterday dreams.

One day you will know
The moments to treasure
Were those you gave up
And didn't stop to measure.

Religion

ANGELS FROM HEAVEN

Dedicated to all of the angels who touched my life

I wish I could have a big thank you party
For all of the angels on earth
That came here from heaven when I needed help
At various times since my birth.
Some stayed many years, some for a month,
Some stayed for only a day.
But I love every one for their caring support,
More than these few words can say.
I think of them often, and I'll always thank God
For all of the angels I knew.
They were a huge blessing and made my life brighter
And one of those angels was you.

GOD'S GIFTS

God gave us brains so we could think,
But instead, we close our mind.
God gave us eyes so we could see,
And yet we're often blind.
God gave us hands so we could work,
But we concentrate on fun.
God gave us feet so we could lead,
But we quit before we're done.
God gave us all these precious gifts
That are so commonly abused.
He gave them to us out of love
And, out of love, they should be used.

THE VOLUNTARY SERVICES

When Saint Peter called for volunteers
To report to Him up high,
The Air Force did not hesitate.
Their home is in the sky.

But when Peter asked for Army scouts,
The troopers plead, "Oh no,
If we can't take our Army tanks,
Please, sir, don't make us go!"

So, Saint Peter called the Navy guys
And heaven made the news
Because the sailors smuggled in
Some pretty girls and booze.

But no Marines were called at all,
And you know the reason why?
If they survived their basic,
They were too tough to die!

CROSSROADS

Will I fill God's plan for me before my life is done?
Did I take the path I'm on to do good for someone?
Did I make a big mistake? Did I listen to God's voice?
If I could change my life now, would I make a better choice?

I think about the crossroads I faced throughout my life
When I moved so far from home and became a wife.
Did I not listen close enough to follow our Lord's plan?
Was my life mapped out for me to choose a different man?

Would I have had a stable home and husband who was true?
Would I have given birth to sons and had a daughter, too?
If I turned left instead of right and chose a different mate,
Would I be alive today or would I have met my fate?

My college years and my careers, the people whom I met,
It appears, throughout the years, are things I don't regret.
If I turned left instead of right, how would my life have
    changed?
Perhaps I'm on the road I'm on 'cause God had it arranged.

WRITING WITH PASSION

I write with passion about child abuse prevention because a
   man grabbed me and held a gun to my head when I was
   five years old.

I write with passion about spouse abuse prevention because
   I saw my father beat my mother and I heard her screams
   for help.

I write with passion about suicide prevention because I
   could not save my good friend and neighbor who took
   her own life.

I write with passion about the struggles of single parents
   because I felt the agony of divorce and raised my sons
   alone.

I write with passion about substance abuse prevention be-
   cause a family member is a recovering addict who nearly
   lost his life.

I write with passion about the value of education because
   I earned my bachelor's degree as a single parent with
   three part-time jobs.

I write with passion about the importance of a work ethic
   because that made it possible for me to reach my goals
   for a better life.

I write with passion about making a difference and helping others because my friends were always there when I needed them most.

I write with passion about setting goals and daring to dream because sometimes goals and dreams might be all we have left.

I write with passion about believing in ourselves, God, and our country because I value my freedom, and I have seen miracles.

I write with passion because I have seen that, been there, heard that, felt that, and all of those moments left a mark in the center of my heart.

I live with passion, and I will not allow anyone to put me down because I'm mighty proud of the person I am in spite of where I have been.

I have been to hell and back, but I thank God for my struggles because they have given me more strength and empathy than most people will ever know.

ODE (OWED) TO TITHING

Dedicated to single parents

I'd sure like to tithe, but what have I got?
My wallet is empty, and my checks would be hot.
I have overdue bills, and I barely paid rental.
My teeth are decayed 'cause I cannot pay dental.
My car is a clunker and broke down yesterday.
So, how can I tithe? How can I tithe, anyway?
My plumbing is leaking, and my dishwasher died.
To endure such dilemmas, I need Christ at my side.
So, I attend church and say a free prayer,
A place to recover, but even in there
God needs my money and that isn't funny.
The Lord's house must also pay dues.
So, please ask the preacher about a new feature:
Would Jesus accept IOUs?

Family I came from

Family

Family I had

THE PREGNANCY BLUES

When you discovered you were pregnant
And your clothes were getting tight,
I bet you could have kicked yourself
For messing up that night.

When your tummy got so big around
You waddled like a duck,
I bet you never dreamed such fun
Could bring such awful luck.

When you went into the Labor Room
While enduring so much pain,
I bet you thought you'd give up sex
'Cause this was just insane.

But when the moment finally came
That you held your baby near,
I bet you were so thrilled and proud
You'll mess up again next year!

Me with my first-born son, Shawn, in 1971

MARTHA

Her graduation day
At the young-old age nineteen,
It was her graduation,
Not the usual kind you've seen.

Her teeth decayed into her gums,
Her jaw heavy from the puss,
Perhaps the infection numbed her brain
And she could have been like us.

I heard her agonizing cry
Ring in my ears at night.
A young and frightened child myself,
I could not make it right.

She was helpful, kind, and cheerful,
But she's "retarded," they all said.
So, ignored and usually hidden,
She died alone in bed.

Her graduation day
In gray coffin and black hearse.
It was her graduation
And we celebrate the curse.

THE WAKE

Her young body lies in sweet repose,
Like a picture on a wall.
Resembling a life,
But she isn't there at all.

Her cold face is white and empty,
All her fears and pain have gone.
Her struggles are now finished,
And her spirit traveled on.

What cruel lesson, I must ask you,
Or what reason could be Thine?
The purpose of her life
I seek, but I cannot find.

THE TERRIBLE TRUTH

Dedicated to my sons

If you do something naughty,
And your parents ask you why.
Remember that a bad truth
Is better than a lie.
Telling them a good lie
Might work for you today
But chances are you will be caught
Somewhere along the way.
So, always tell the terrible truth
I know it's hard to do.
But when you wear an honest face,
It sure looks good on you!

DADDY'S TIME

Dedicated to Shawn and Ryan

I know …
It's Daddy's time,
Your special time to be
with your very own daddy.
So, I let you go
With an approving smile
On my face and
Nod of my head.
I will not impose
My hurt upon you,
My innocent children.

I know …
You can love Daddy.
It is not a threat
To your warm and special
Feelings of love for me.
I understand,
And it's okay.
Enjoy your time to be
With your very own daddy,
My dear, sweet children.

You know …
I'm happy for you.
Happy to know that
You feel secure in my love,
Secure enough to run out the door
Without stopping for a hug.
You know I'll always be here
Waiting for you …
When it's Mommy's time.
Your special time to be
With your very own mommy!

My sons Shawn and Ryan with their dad,
the late Franklin R. Harvey

WHEN DRUCILLA DIED

Dedicated to the late Drucilla Vargas.

When Drucilla died
I broke down and cried.
I thought I'd be relieved
Because she made me peeved
With long and frequent calls
Of heartache, pain and falls.
She often made a scene
And was a Drama Queen.
So I thought it wasn't real
And didn't know how to feel.
I did not comprehend
That she was near the end.
But she made us all aware
She needed lots of care.
I told her to hang tough
But that was not enough.
She lost her will to live
Had no more fight to give.
Her joy in life was gone

So it's good she traveled on
To her eternal home
Where she'll never be alone.
But oh, what I wouldn't do
To once again see Dru
Or hear from her again.
I'd help her with a grin.
It's only been a while
And now I miss her smile.
When younger and still strong
Before her health went wrong.
She loved to cook and clean.
Best food you've ever seen,
And share good family days.
Now gone, I'm in a haze,
Left here on earth to grieve
Because she had to leave.
And when Drucilla died,
We all broke down and cried.

TOO LATE

Dedicated to my sons

Wait a minute.
Maybe later.
You're in my way.
Don't interrupt.
I'm too busy.
Just go and play.

Your senior prom?
Oh no, my child,
Leaving in May!
Grown so fast,
I don't know you.
But can't you stay?

I'll listen now.
Please sit, let's talk.
What did you say?
You don't have time.
It's much too late.
Some other day?

My granddaughter, Crystal, 2, on Santa's lap.

Seasons

*Four old ladies, all over age 70, visiting Santa: Judi Mann, Trish Palmer,
Barbara Sellers, and Sally Drexler*

THE CHRISTMAS SPIRIT

I recall a Christmas past
When I thought I'd be the last
To ever feel down and low
With all the Christmas lights aglow.
But now alone, I felt so sad.
On Christmas day, we should be glad.
Could it be the missing snow?
I asked myself, but I didn't know.
I just knew I wore a frown.
The Christmas spirit let me down.

I thought I'd cheer up in the stores
With Christmas shoppers by the scores.
But I just saw them push and shove.
I really didn't see any love.
I used to see it everywhere.
I think the spirit's hiding there.
Yes, Christmas time should always bring
A feeling that will make us sing.
But that year, I just wore a frown.
The Christmas spirit let me down.

THE FALL OF AUTUMN

I can see branches now,
The clear branches of trees
Once hidden by the leaves
Scattered across the fields.

When the first snowflakes fall,
And the freezing wind hovers,
I reach for more covers
And resist getting up.

I shiver, teeth chatter.
With bare bottom and feet
Balancing near the heat,
I awkwardly get dressed.

I melt a window spot
With the palm of my hand.
The icicles look grand
Decorating the eves.

Jack Frost originals,
Perfect distribution
Natures contribution
That justifies the cold.

CLASS REUNION

As class reunions come and go,
We're bound to see some change, you know.
But most of us look just the same,
And I remember every name.
Well, not every, but a lot …
Only sixty I forgot.

Many years gone; what a shame!
What was lost and what was gained?
Just the hair on someone's head,
And some extra pounds to shed.
But Father Time did not erase
The youthful look upon each face.

Such lack of sleep, such wear-and-tear,
Yet not a wrinkle anywhere—
Except around the chin and eyes
That some of us can still disguise.
So, here we are. What can we say?
It almost seems like yesterday.

Our hometown teachers were the best,
But we all had to do the rest.
A brand-new car and our own house,
A great career and loving spouse,
And children that are never bad—
Just like the ones our parents had.

So, our dearest plans and dreams
Now have been achieved it seems—
Except a few, and that's okay
'Cause we're not finished anyway.

Yeah, many years have passed somehow.
We're all adults and wiser now.
And through experience we have learned
That true success is really earned—
Not handed-out on silver platters.

But tell your children hard work matters.
"With any luck," declare young scholars
"I'll make an easy million dollars!"

HAPPY NEW YEAR

Every time the New Year comes,
We look upon our past,
With highest hopes the year ahead
Is better than the last.

We make New Year's resolutions
To do this and to do that,
But soon it's very evident
We all talked through our hat.

We can claim some years are good
And other years are poor.
Yet, the kind of year we usually get,
Is the kind we're working for.

So, let's all make this coming year
The best one that we've had,
The kind of year that when it leaves
We may not be so glad!

Character Sketches

Character sketch by Donna Louise Turrentine

RUPERT THE RAT

Rupert the rat,
An adulterous male,
Let all his brains
Fall down in his tail.
To get back his youth,
He went out to swing.
He left a good wife
For a pretty young thing.
No one believed
He would take it so far.
But he dressed like a rocker,
Bought a sports car,
And danced every night
With his cute little honey,
'Til she left him alone
When he ran out of money.

LOOSE LUCILLE

Loose Lucille
Has sex appeal
And a body that she flaunts.
It's the only way
She ever learned
To get the things she wants.

ANOREXIC KIM

Anorexic Kim
Is way too slim.
And now she's getting thinner.
She eats yogurt for brunch
And nothing for lunch
And only drinks water for dinner.

TWO-TON PETE

Two-ton Pete
Loves to eat.
He pigs out every hour.
Then after that,
He prays his fat
Will come off in the shower .

MIXED-UP ROSE

Poor mixed-up Rose.
God only knows
Which man she will marry or call.
Bill, Richard, and Jack
Keep taking her back,
And she swears her true love to them all!

GRUDGE-HOLDING DICK

Grudge-holding Dick
Makes himself sick.
He'll hate you until he is dead.
As long as you live,
He will not forgive
His brains are a vendetta red.

POSITIVE SUE

Positive Sue
Never stays blue.
She smiles and laughs through the day.
No matter what's wrong,
She still sings a song
And chases her doldrums away.

NEGATIVE JOE

Negative Joe
Will never let go
Of pain, hurt, and sorrow in life.
And what's really bad:
He loves feeling sad,
Which adds to his anger and strife.

SHOPPING SHERRIE

Shopping Sherrie
Wants to marry
The wealthiest man in town.
'Cause there's no end
To what she'll spend,
And her credit is going down.

STINGY CHUCK

Stingy Chuck
Saves every buck
And counts every dime and penny.
He never gives
Expensive gifts
In fact, he does not give any.

TRAVELING JENNY

Brave, traveling Jenny
I doubt that there's any
Place in this world she won't know.
She simply delights
In seeing new sites.
She'll pack up her bags and just go.

STAY-AT-HOME DOUG

Stay-at-home Doug,
Snug as a bug,
He never leaves home out of fear.
He won't take a plane
Or ride on a train
And hasn't left town in a year.

PERFECT PAULINE

Perfect Pauline
Is not really mean.
Just a know it all right to the letter.
Sure, she puts people down
And will boss you around,
But how else can she prove that she's better?

DECEITFUL JIM

Deceitful Jim
Acts on a whim
And he seldom does anything right.
He's such a jerk
He claims my work
So he can appear to be bright.

That's Life

LABELS

We label each other
Like food in a jar.
Whatever we're labeled
That is what we are!

A loser or winner
A saint or a sinner
A snob or a slob,
Who can't get a job.

We are smart or just dumb
A born champ or a bum.
We are fast or too slow
'Cause someone said so.

Rich class, middle class,
Wrong side of the track.
Such good and bad labels
Are stuck on our back.

But once we know better,
Then we can choose
The labels we want and
The labels we use.

OCCUPATION PLEASE

I'm a very busy lady.
My work begins at dawn.
I cook and clean the house,
Wash clothes, and mow the lawn.

I'm a telephone operator,
And then what's even more.
I'm a butler in disguise,
Answering my front door.

I'm a full-time taxi driver,
Take my kids to school and shop.
And when the darlings misbehave
I'm the jury, judge, and cop.

I give my children each a bath,
Shampoo their little heads.
Then I read them story books
And tuck them in their beds.

I'm the family accountant,
Pay the bills and write our friends.
Unlike so many normal jobs,
My workday never ends.

But whenever someone asks me,
"What's your occupation, please?"
I have so many titles.
They don't have time for these.

So, in spite of my many roles
And dedicated life,
I'm forced to meekly answer,
"Oh, I'm just a housewife."

CHOICES

We make our own choices.
Some make us happy,
And some make us sad.
Some turn out good,
And some turn out bad.

We can't change our choices.
As we get older
And gain more hindsight,
We cannot go back
To make our wrongs right.

We have but one chance
To make our lives shine.
Then you're stuck with yours,
And I'm stuck with mine.

LEGACY

What's one good lesson that I learned in life
That I'd like to share with all others?
Perhaps I might say to laugh, sing, and dance
And cherish your sisters and brothers.

If all else is gone, and we must go on,
It's important to be strong at heart.
So, I must agree to believe in yourself
Is a mighty fine place we should start.

But some people think that to be satisfied,
They must focus on their selfish greed.
But if we neglect our family and friends,
We'll be lonely and empty indeed.

Life is a journey that comes to an end.
What will our legacy be?
When we say good-bye, will anyone cry?
Will anyone really miss me?

DETERMINISM

Our desires: fantasy
Our password: rules.
Our future: destiny
Our surname: fools.

DECEPTION

Danger and destruction signs
Might confuse us with a name.
Some labels could be changing,
While the contents are the same.

You may call liver "candy,"
But that would not change the taste.
The label will look dandy
But it still might go to waste.

So, better not unlock a cage
That someone labeled "kitten."
You could find a lion's den
And be severely bitten.

ARE YOU RICH?

Sometimes we look down on the poor
And cater to the rich.
But do we ever really know
Which one of them is which?

If you never held a baby
Or never climbed a tree,
If you never made somebody laugh,
You're not as rich as me.

You may own a couple houses,
Cars, diamonds, odds, and ends,
But none of this will mean a thing,
If you don't have true friends.

When wealth becomes our only love,
Is it really worth the price?
Does it truly matter what we have
Or what we sacrifice?

What's the worth of a faithful spouse?
The worth of perfect health?
What's the worth of a loving heart?
And peace within yourself?

Sometimes the poor are mighty rich,
And the wealthy are still poor.
Are you rich? That all depends
On what you're living for.

PART II

Short Stories

Hand pump *like the one my mother used to get water when we had no running water in the house.*

The Forbidden Rock

Secluded farm with a windmill like my parents had when this story took place.

IT WAS 1951, and we were still living on our farm in Braham, Minnesota, which had woods on two sides. Like many farm families in those days, we were dependent on our windmill to generate power for indoor lights and running water. We had no phone, and our nearest neighbor lived about two miles away.

Without strong winds, our lights often flickered or went out completely. When that happened, Ma usually lit the candles she made out of beeswax, but sometimes we all sat in the dark while she told us spooky ghost stories.

One hot summer day, Pa went to South St. Paul to sell a truckload of pigs. This was one of those times we had no running water in the house. When we had no running water in our house, Ma used an old-fashioned hand pump outside. This time, however, the handle on the pump was broken, and she needed some water to boil potatoes for supper. So, she decided to remove the "forbidden rock." I called it that because Ma had forbidden us to move it.

My younger sister Ann and I often ran around the outside of our stucco farmhouse playing tag, and that big rock was in our way, so I asked Ann to help me move it. When Ma looked out the window and saw what we were doing, she ran out of the house, grabbed us away from the rock, and scolded us saying, "No, no, no! You must never move that rock!"

I doubt we could have even budged it because it was really huge, and we were just two little girls. I was four years old, and Ann was three. I wondered, however, what was under that rock. In my four-year-old mind, I remember thinking a fire-breathing dragon might live in a cave there. Whatever it was, I could tell from Ma's voice that it was something very dangerous, so I was very surprised when she decided to move it.

As all of us kids gathered around the "forbidden rock," our mother explained that it covered an old, abandoned well, and if she moved that rock and the water level was high enough, she might be able to get some water to boil potatoes for dinner. While the older kids sat nearby, she told me it was my job to keep Ann and our younger brother Mark away from the well so they would not accidentally fall in. So, I took them each by the hand and just stood back and watched.

Stretching out onto the grass, my mother reached down with her long-handled pan, while my nine-year-old brother Tom sat close by holding a flashlight. The hole in the ground was not very big around but apparently the water level must have been deceiving. Ma asked my siblings Bernie, eight; Pat, seven; and Rose six, to help hold her legs down so she could inch herself forward just a little farther and reach deeper into the well.

Suddenly my mother slipped, and I heard her scream as she fell into the well. A few seconds later, we heard our mother's voice. Somehow, she managed to grab onto a ladder that partially lined the inside of the well, but she could not get herself back up because it did not extend to the top .

While clinging to the ladder upside down, our mother asked Tom to run to the nearby shed to get a rope. He quickly tied one end of the rope around a nearby tree and threw the other end down to our mother. But she could not get herself turned around to grab hold of the rope and pull herself up.

Luckily, Tom was fairly big and strong for his age. He already knew how to make slip knots, so he quickly made a slip knot at one end of the rope to loop around my mother's legs while Bernie tied the other end to the back of the nearby tractor hinge. My memory is a little fuzzy exactly how they ended up getting the slip knot secured around my mother's legs because I was not standing close enough to see that part very well.

However, I remember what happened next as clearly as if it happened yesterday. Tom and Bernie had never before started the tractor by themselves, but they knew what to do, and they did it. The tractor had a crank on the front of it. While Tom turned the crank on the front of the tractor, Bernie sat on the tractor seat and adjusted the choke. As soon as they got the tractor started, Tom got on the tractor and slowly let up on the clutch. He knew he had to take it easy, or the tractor could jerk to a stop.

I watched as the tractor moved forward, and they pulled our mother to safety just in the nick of time. She could not have held on much longer. Her hair got wet, but other than that, she was okay.

I rushed over to give Ma a hug. A few moments later, we heard a crackling sound, followed by a rumble and hollow, echoing splash. The old, water-soaked wooden ladder had just broken off. The ladder that no one knew existed until that night seemed to have been there for the soul purpose of saving our mother's life. Now, this purpose having been fulfilled, it was no longer needed.

That evening, when Pa returned home from the city, Ma told him at the supper table what happened and how my older brothers had rescued her from drowning in the well.

"Good job!" he said to Tom. "You did a really good job!"

Then he said to Ma, "We have some really smart kids!"

That was it. Nothing more was said. Earlier that day, I had witnessed my older brothers and sisters, only ages six to nine, saving Ma's life, and I said to my four-year-old self, "Is that all there is? Is that all the thanks they get for rescuing our mother from the well?"

But at least it was something I would never forget because I permanently recorded it in my memory. It amazes me that I have been blessed with such a good memory that I can even recall several details about my life back as far as age 2. From what I have read that is very unusual. It surprises me that many people cannot remember much of anything before age 5, and I remember lots of things my older sisters and brothers have long forgotten.

Looking back, I don't know why Ma didn't tie a rope to the handle of a bucket such as a milk pail and lower it into the well with a rope to dip it into the water and bring it back up instead. But Ma did not grow up on a farm. She was a commercial fisherman's daughter so she knew a lot about fishing, but she was not too farm-smart yet when it came to the best ways of doing things.

At that time, Ma already had seven living children and she lived to have six more. She had a total of 14 children, but Katherine had already passed away at three months. Throughout the years, Ma had several more near-death experiences, but it was not in the cards for her to die young. In fact, she lived to be 93.

Now when I think about how such young children so bravely and miraculously saved our mother's life, I know that if something like that were to happen today, it would be all over the news. To our parents, however, my older brothers and sisters simply did what they were expected to do.

I tried to imagine what would happen if I fell into a well and called to my sons for help. They would probably have responded by saying, "Not now," Mom. "Just hold on. We will help you during commercial or after we finish playing our video game."

Not that my sons do not love me, but it is just a very different kind of life now indeed!

A bull similar to this charged at me, and I barely escaped under an electric barbed wire fence.

Orgie the Friendly Bull

Aerial view of the farm I was living on when this story took place. This photo was taken by the Pope Country Tribune in 1954.

WOULD YOU BE A fool and trust a bull? Knowing what I know now, my answer would be, "No, not me!"

Pa most likely had more than two bulls throughout his farming career, but I only remember two of them: Herbie and Orgie. Herbie was all black and really big and dangerous looking.

Anyone could tell Herbie was definitely a bull that nobody would mess with if you valued your life. Orgie was big also, but he was brownish-red like all of the other steers and cows in the barnyard so it was a little more difficult to identify him as a bull.

When I was nine years old, it was my after-school job to run a few miles out to the pasture where the cows were grazing and chase them back to the barn in time to be milked that evening.

Because I was just a young girl, I could not yet tell the difference between a cow and a plain old steer. If Pa had Holstein cows, I certainly would have known which ones were cows because everyone knows black and white four-legged animals are cows. Even the city kids knew that. But Pa did not have Holstein cows. No, for some reason Pa only had Shorthorn cows, and they were all the same color as the other steers: brownish-red. None of my older brothers or anyone in the family ever bothered to point out the difference to me. I wasn't worried about it though. All I had to do was get them to the barn in time. Therefore, if it had four legs, I chased it home and the rest took care of itself.

Once I chased all the four-legged animals to the barn, the cows knew they were cows, so they automatically went to their assigned stanchions where they belonged. Then Pa or my brothers would walk around and lock them in place before they were hooked up to milking machines.

Usually, it did not take very long to get the cows to start moving in the right direction. I only had to yell a few commanding cow words at them to get them into the lane to go home.

I just hollered, "Go, Bossy, go!" or "Go home, Bossy, go!" That usually worked really well, but sometimes I also had to say, "Shoo-wey, shoo-wey" or throw a few stones at them to show I meant business.

One night when I went out to the pasture to chase the cows home, they ignored me and continued to eat grass. No matter how many cow names I yelled, none of them would budge. They all acted like they had taken stubborn cow pills or something. Pretty soon, I started to worry that I would be in serious trouble and might even get my butt whipped if I failed to get those cows home in time.

Then I noticed that one cow in particular seemed to be in charge of all the others. Therefore, I figured if I could get THAT one to move, all the rest would follow. So, I picked up some bigger stones and started to throw them at the leader of the pack.

Suddenly, I realized I must be dealing with a neurotic cow because it did something no other cow ever did. It reared around with its head down, dug its hoofs into the dirt and looked like it was getting ready to charge straight at me.

At that point, I decided to drop my stones and beat feet as fast as I could for the electric barbed wire fence. That was a very good decision because I barely scrambled under the fence when that neurotic cow butted its head right into it. I thanked God that electric fence was there to save me.

While I was busy running for my life, I noticed that all the other cows had already headed for home, so I decided to leave that crazy one behind, hoping Pa would not miss it.

That night at the supper table, Pa said, "Oh, by the way, Barb, I got a new bull today that I put out in the pasture with the cows, so you better be a little more careful from now on when you go out there to chase the cows home."

So, the neurotic cow was actually a dangerous bull!

Great! That's just great that Pa decided to tell me after I already came so close to getting attacked or killed.

I never told Pa about the dangerous encounter I had with that bull, but I was still surprised when Pa started calling that bull "Orgie the Friendly Bull." In fact, Pa often said, "Orgie is the friendliest bull in the world. He's like a big, tame pussy cat." Pa told just about everyone he met about "Orgie the Friendly Bull." He even wrote and submitted a story about Orgie to a farming magazine.

In the summer, Pa often led Orgie by a short rope into our front yard where all of us children played. Then he tied his end of the rope to a short stake, pounded it into the ground, and left Orgie there to eat the tall green grass of home. I thought it was safe because I did not know that Orgie could easily have pulled that stake out of the ground.

Ma got really upset when Pa put Orgie in our front yard to eat grass. She complained that none of her neighbor friends would come over to visit anymore. Ma said whenever they saw that bull in the yard, they would just keep on driving by. And if they did stop, they did not dare to get out of their cars and come into the house because they were afraid of that bull. Her friend Mary often said, "Only a fool would trust a bull!" Mary also told Ma, "The children could be in danger with that bull in the yard."

Whenever Ma complained about it, however, Pa just laughed and gave his "Orgie the Friendly Bull" story again. But Ma did not trust that bull either. Whenever Pa put Orgie too close to the clotheslines near the back of the house, Ma stopped hanging our red clothes on the line to dry because she thought the bull would charge at the color red. Of course, like all other cattle, bulls are colorblind to the color red, and therefore, it has no influence whatsoever on the bull's behavior. In fact, it's only the movement of a matador's cape (not the color red) that irritates a bull enough to charge. But Ma did not know that, so she sorted out all the red clothes, and our red clothes never got washed again until Pa put that bull back into the barn for the winter.

One night while Pa was inside the pen in the barn with "Orgie the Friendly Bull," he decided to play a little teasing game with the bull. As he was feeding Orgie some hay, he used his pitchfork to lightly scratch Orgie on the back. It was Pa's way of petting the bull. However, Orgie did not like being scratched on the back with the pitchfork.

Suddenly, Orgie charged at Pa and pinned him against the barn wall. Pa yelled for help, but my brothers had already finished their chores and gone back into the house. In Pa's struggle to get free from the bull's hold, he pulled on the ring in Orgie's nose, which caused the bull to back off. Then Pa finally managed to get out of the pen. When Pa reached the house, he collapsed on the kitchen floor in a pool of blood. Pa did make a full recovery from the penetrated wound Orgie made in his side, but Pa never again bragged about "Orgie the Friendly Bull."

After that, Pa stubbornly continued to stake Orgie in our front yard to eat grass, but I noticed that instead of leading the bull with only a short rope, Pa used a much longer rope and kept his eyes on Orgie the whole time. And instead of using a short stake to anchor Orgie to the ground, Pa used a much bigger, stronger-looking stake that would be a lot more difficult for Orgie to pull up.

Moral of this true story: Don't be a fool and trust a bull!

A Special
Kind of Lipstick

SOMETIMES WHEN THE CATHOLIC priest spoke to high school students, he said, "The only way to prevent pregnancy is through abstinence." But I didn't think it worked very well because my parents were obstinate, and they had 14 children.

Whenever I asked my mother questions about pregnancy, she simply said, "All you need to know, young lady, is to never allow a boy to kiss you because that's how you get pregnant."

When I persisted with more questions, she said. "What you don't know can't hurt you!"

My mother had a saying for everything, but I never liked that one because I didn't think it was true.

When I was in seventh grade, a male classmate tried to kiss me in English class. I remembered what my mother said, so I kicked him. I was wearing soft-toed shoes so yikes that hurt! In fact, my entire big toenail turned black and fell off. However, that poor student was limping around for two weeks. He never tried that stupid kissing thing again.

We didn't have a TV until my Uncle Bernie gave us one for Christmas when I was in fourth grade. My father made strict rules on what we could and could not watch.

"You cannot watch any programs that have shooting, cursing, or kissing in them," he said.

That pretty much left Lawrence Welk and the weather report.

When my father was working out in the fields or went to south St. Paul, Minnesota, with a truckload of animals for market, my mother would turn on the TV and watch her favorite soap opera, *General Hospital*. I noticed one actress did a lot of kissing in that program, but she never got pregnant. So, I asked my older sister Pat, "How come that actress can do so much kissing and never get pregnant?"

Pat looked at me with a straight face and said, "Oh, that's because she wears a special kind of lipstick!"

Wow! I wanted to get myself some of that special kind of lipstick so I would not have to worry about getting pregnant. I looked at all of the lipsticks on display in our local Potter's Five and Dime store, but I could not find it. I was really disappointed, but I was sure they would carry it in the big city. So, after I graduated from high school and moved to St. Paul, I started looking for it again.

You've probably heard of girls who turned "sweet 16 and never been kissed." Well, I turned sweet 16, 17, 18, and 19 before I was ever kissed. I was not about to allow any boy to kiss me until I found that special kind of lipstick.

It would have helped if I knew what it was called. I thought it might be something like "Pink Protection" or "Red Rubber," but whenever I asked store clerks about it, they always gave me strange looks and said, "Never heard of it."

When I was 19, a guy I met in the greeting card section of a drug store asked me to go bowling. He seemed like such a nice guy I decided to take my chances. But before going on my first date I wanted to be strong in the Lord, so I decided to go to a Catholic church up on the hill.

"I'm going to go to confession at that Catholic church up on the hill," I told my roommate who shared her apartment with me. She grew up in the same hometown as me on another farm.

"Oh no, don't go there!" she said. "You should wait until you go home on a weekend and go to confession there instead."

"Why?" I asked. "One Catholic church is just like another Catholic church, right?"

"Okay, but don't say I didn't warn you," she said.

Warn me about what? I wondered. She did not tell me that the Catholic priests in big cities are used to hearing some extremely hot confessions and she knew that would not be the kind of confession I would be giving.

When I finished confessing what I thought was a long list of sins, the big-city priest started asking me questions I was never asked before. His questions and my answers went like this:

"How old are you?"

"Nineteen, Father."

"Didn't you leave something out of your confession?"

"No, Father, not that I know of."

"Do you have a boyfriend?"

"Yes, Father, I just got one."

"Did you have intercourse?"

"What's that?" I had to ask because I never heard that word before, and I didn't know what it meant.

At that moment, I heard a thud like the priest might have passed out. I wondered if he had a heart attack and needed medical help. For the longest time, I tried to figure out what I should do. I could not leave the confessional because the priest had not yet given me my penance and absolution for my sins.

After a long silence, the priest finally spoke again.

"You are not from around here, are you?"

"No, Father, I grew up on a farm in a small town."

Next, he gave me some instructions that went like this:

"I want you to go home and ask your mother to tell you about the birds and the bees."

"Why, Father? I already know a lot about bees because my father is a beekeeper."

"Just go home and ask your mother where babies come from," he said.

Then the priest gave me the smallest penance I had ever received, the shortest prayer in the Catholic religion: one "Glory Be."

I could not believe it! One "Glory Be" a 10-second prayer for all those sins! In my hometown, the priest would have socked it to me. I would have been on my knees praying the entire rosary for a whole hour. Going to confession in the big city was not so bad, after all.

I was so happy with my short penance that as I walked back to my apartment, I sang *"Ava Maria"* out loud.

I was slender, and my long hair was blowing in the breeze. It was the first time I was dressed in a new blue suit, high heels, and nylons. I felt happy and beautiful.

Suddenly, as I passed a motel, a man jumped out in front of me with a fist full of money. For some strange reason, he wanted to give it to me. I knew I was singing extra good, but I didn't know I was singing that well.

"No. You keep your money. I'm glad you like my singing, but I'm singing for free today, so I don't want your money," I said.

As I continued walking, the man followed me and kept pulling out more money and more money.

"No," I insisted. "Keep your money. I don't want your money. I really cannot take your money."

When I finally got back to the apartment, I told my roommate about the strange man who was trying to give me a whole bunch of free money.

"Oh, my, God!" she said. "What street did you walk back on?"

"Concord. Why?"

"Don't you know that's where the prostitutes hang out?"

"Prostitutes? What's that?" I asked.

It was the first time I ever heard that word, too.

My girlfriend handed me a book and said, "Read it!" When I found out what a prostitute was, I sure was glad I did not take that money.

The following weekend, I went home for a visit to see my parents and all my younger brothers and sisters.

"Mom, I'm 19 years old, and the Catholic priest in St. Paul told me I should ask you where babies come from."

My mother looked surprised and said, "You know, the stork brought you!"

"Mom, no bird in the world would be so stupid that it would drop 14 babies here and only one at the farm down the road!" I said.

Looking back on my first experiences as a naïve, good-looking, slender young country girl in a big city, I believe a guardian angel must have been protecting me because I sure did not know much about how to protect myself.

What we don't know can hurt us!

Risky Dating

The late Erma Courtney was my former neighbor and good friend who went to the restaurant to check out my date. She just might have helped save my life.

IF I HAD KNOWN I was in a car with one of the most prolific serial killers in history, I might have been too afraid to move—frozen in place and unable to defend myself. But I just thought the handsome stranger who offered me a ride was about to get fresh with me, and I never had any problem defending my honor and protecting my virginity. So, I slipped off my high-heel shoe, whacked him a good hard one between the legs, jumped out of the car, ran to the nearest house, and rang the doorbell. Thank God the homeowners immediately came to the door, and when the young man saw that, he quickly drove away.

I knew I should never have accepted a ride with a stranger. My mother often told me that, but after stepping out of a beauty salon I missed my bus, and I needed to get to the downtown bank before it closed. I promised my cousin Christy that I would go to a movie with her that evening, and I needed to get more money because my hairdo cost more than I anticipated.

That's when a handsome, charming man pulled up in a new cream-colored Volkswagen Beetle and kindly offered me a ride.

"I see you missed your bus," he said with a beaming smile on his face. "I'm headed that way, so I can give you a ride. Just tell me where you want to go."

He looked like such a nice, harmless fellow, so I took a chance, and he drove me straight to the bank and dropped me off. What surprised me is that when I came out of the bank, he was still there, parked in front of the bank. He offered to give me a ride back home.

At that point I was a little hesitant, but I also had a little more confidence that this guy was perfectly safe because, after all, he had already taken me to where I wanted to go with no problem. So, I got in, and he started driving back to the area where he picked me up.

I was 21, a slender brunette with long hair, and I had just moved to Tacoma, Washington, where Theodore (Ted) Bundy was living at the time. In fact, Bundy, who was three months younger than me, was very familiar with the neighborhood in which I was living because he grew up in Tacoma and graduated from Woodrow Wilson High School, the school my cousin Christy (whose family I lived with) attended. After Bundy graduated from high school, he attended the University of Puget Sound, the college I later attended.

When I had my encounter with Bundy, however, it was only 1968. Bundy didn't start killing women until five or six years later—at least not that we know of. That does not mean I could not have become his first victim. The mere thought of it still sends chills up my spine.

As Bundy got near the neighborhood where I lived, he drove past where I asked him to turn. That's when red flags went up in my mind, and I knew I might be in trouble. I figured my best hope to get away from this guy would be while he was still driving slowly through neighborhood side streets.

That's also when I remembered what my mother often told me: "Whenever you go out, wear high heels. If a guy tries to get fresh with you, you can slip off your high heel, hold on to the toe and whack him between the legs with the heel."

So that's what I did. When I started whacking him, he immediately pulled the car over to a stop. Before he could grab me, I had already jumped out, hoping he would not run after me.

I never knew how lucky I was to have escaped unharmed from a would-be serial killer, however, until several years later when I saw Bundy's face and his 1968 Volkswagen Beetle all over the news. By that time, I was already married and had a son. Since I was no longer a single available young lady, I felt grateful that I would never face the prospect of accepting a ride from a stranger again.

Some news reporters pointed out that nearly all of Bundy's murdered victims looked enough alike to be sisters. Knowing I fit the same physical description of the women Bundy killed—mostly brunettes with long hair—also gave me the chills.

According to what I heard on the news, Bundy eventually admitted to killing 30 women between 1973 and 1978 across seven states. Some accounts say Bundy killed women across 11 states, and he might have killed 100 women or more. That was never proven, however. Because Bundy was executed in Florida's electric chair in 1989 to pay for his crimes, we might never know for sure.

It surprises me that many serial killers maintain a "loving" relationship with a woman or even get married to a woman while actively killing other women. For example, Bundy had a six-year relationship with a woman he met in Seattle and played the role of stepfather to her daughter from a previous relationship. Both the mother and daughter said they loved Bundy and were completely shocked when they learned about his secret killings.

Even more surprising is that Ann Rule, author of the 1980 true-crime novel *The Stranger Beside Me*, worked with Bundy during the late shift at the Seattle Suicide Crisis Center, yet she never suspected that he was the serial killer she was writing about. As a former police officer with the Seattle Police Department, Rule was very familiar with police work.

Rule passed away July 26, 2015, but she wrote more than 30 true crime books. I have many autographed copies because

I attended several of her speaking and book signing engagements in this local area.

Rule said that even after evidence started coming out proving Bundy was the serial killer, at first she could not believe the nice, charming, intelligent young man she worked with could possibly be capable of being the serial killer.

In one of her presentations, Rule said Bundy had sawed off the inside passenger's door handle so his victims could not escape.

I often wondered if it was my fault Bundy did that because I was able to escape from his car when the inside car door handle was still there.

In 1981, I went through an unexpected divorce from my first husband after 12 years of marriage and became a single parent. Then in 1982, I graduated from the University of Puget Sound and started actively dating again—the same year Tacoma and Seattle had a new serial killer who started strangling women in his home.

Rule also wrote a book about him, the Green River killer, Gary Ridgway, who committed the majority of his murders from 1982 to 1984, but Ridgway continued killing women until 1998 because it took so long for him to be caught.

I just now read that Ridgway, who held a job as a truck painter at the Kenworth Truck Plant in Renton (suburb between Tacoma and Seattle), was "obsessed with not getting caught" so he did not want to take any chances by killing victims that might put the police on his trail.

That's why he mostly killed prostitutes and/or other women who might not be missed for several days or weeks.

Most of the time I only dated men I met through Parents Without Partners (PWP), Bible studies, or Toastmasters International—men I knew fairly well over a period of time.

Online dating was not yet available, but sometimes I got dates through personal ads in local newspapers.

In 1982, I was dating Patrick Molloy, a full-blooded Irishman I met at a PWP dance, and I dated him for several years. One day after we broke up, I had a dinner date set up with a new guy who was two years older than me at an Italian spaghetti restaurant, located only about three blocks from where I lived. I told Erma, my best friend and next-door neighbor, about my upcoming date, and she offered to go over there at the same time with her friend Kathy so they could check this guy out. Erma often gave me good advice and protected me like a mother hen.

I made sure I sat at a table within viewing distance of Erma and her friend. My date seemed like a really nice fellow, and we had a good conversation. When we were done eating, he said he would like me to go with him to his place so I could meet his three-year-old son who was with a babysitter. I thought if his son was with a babysitter, it should be safe enough, so I foolishly accepted his invitation. While I was in his car on the way over there, however, I started feeling uneasy because I didn't really know him very well yet and I began to wonder if perhaps he didn't even have a son. That's when I decided to tell him about my neighbor and friend who were watching us at the restaurant.

"Did you notice the two ladies in the restaurant sitting across from us?" I asked. "Well, that was actually my neighbor and her friend. They were checking you out. She's always overprotecting me, and I think she even wrote down your license plate number just in case anything happened to me. Isn't that funny?"

No, to my surprise he did not think it was funny. Instead, my date immediately slammed on his brakes to slow down enough to catch the next exit. Then he said something I'll never forget.

"You're the wrong one. I'm taking you back!"

As strange as "you're the wrong one" sounded at the time, I never gave it any more thought until now. When I read that Ridgway was "obsessed with not getting caught" I remembered the strange reaction I got when I told that guy that he was being watched. I looked up old photos of Ridgeway, and he definitely looked like the same guy I met at that restaurant. I'll probably never know for sure, but now I wonder if he was actually the Green River killer. If so, my good friend Erma might have saved my life.

Like Bundy, Ridgway also had a normal, loving relationship at the same time he was out killing other women. In fact, Ridgway had been married three times, but two of his marriages took place before he became a serial killer. He was married to Claudia Barrows from 1970 to 1972 and Marcia Lorene Brown from 1973 to 1981. After Ridgway started his killing spree in 1982, he was married to his third wife, Judith Lynch, from 1988 to 2002. She did not leave him until a year after he was arrested, November. 30, 2001, when DNA connected him to four murders.

By the time Ridgway was convicted on December 18, 2003, he received 48 consecutive life sentences with no possibility of parole. After he went to prison, however, Ridgway was convicted of another murder for a total of at least 49, making him the second most prolific serial killer in American history. To avoid the death penalty, Ridgway pled guilty to 48 of his murders, and he agreed to tell police where the bodies were located so the victims' families could have closure. According to news accounts, however, he actually admitted to killing at least 71 women. Now at age 77 he is still serving his sentences at the Washington State Penitentiary.

By the time Ridgway was caught, I was already married to my second husband, retired Lieutenant Colonel Don Sellers, who I met at my Toastmaster's club. After five years of dating and 10 years of marriage, we got divorced mainly due to problems with my son Ryan, an alcohol and drug addict. My former husband, Don, is 13 years older than me, and I decided he deserved to live out his senior years in peace and quiet. I, on the other hand, was not yet willing to give up on Ryan because I know what a highly intelligent, skilled, and good hard-working young man he could be when clean and sober. Sadly, many addicts like Ryan are never able to find their way back to sobriety, and their addictions destroy more lives than their own. It affects the lives of all of the addict's loved ones, too, but that's another story.

I have been single again now for about 19 years, but my days of risky dating are over. When I was younger, I always thought I was a good judge of character, and I believed that I would know a serial killer if I met one, but I was wrong. Serial killers are masters of disguise. The Green River killer was even able to pass a polygraph test, which is why he was able to remain free to continue killing women over a span of nearly two decades until DNA testing was developed.

When I worked at the Family Counseling Center, I remember reading a book about serial killers, which said they seldom kill people they know and the better they know you, the less likely it is that they will kill you because then you become a human being, a real person with value. That's why serial killers are much more likely to kill prostitutes who are complete strangers. Perhaps they are then able to view them as worthless objects instead.

It's still impossible for me to understand how serial killers are able to live double lives and maintain a loving relationship with a girlfriend or wife, while committing such horrible crimes in secret at the same time. How does one woman become a wife while other women become victims? That mystery might never be solved.

I know one thing for sure: During my younger years of risky dating, I got lucky. It's nothing short of a miracle that I'm still here. I wonder if it was the power of prayer that made the difference. My mother strongly believed in the power of prayer, and she told me that she always prayed for the safety of all of her children. Perhaps I'll never know just how much difference her prayers made in my life or if they helped save my life .

*This is the kind of dial phone I had at
the time this story took place.*

Calling Long Distance

*My son Shawn as a toddler, holding a black
dial phone like the one I had in this story.*

THE PHONE RANG. I looked at my watch. It was 1:30 a.m.

I hated getting calls this late at night. It usually meant someone died, and I still had not yet gotten over the recent death of my older friend Joy. I called her my "West Coast mother" because she treated me like a daughter ever since we met when I was looking for a job here. We quickly formed a tight bond and kept in touch all throughout my husband's military moves up and down the East Coast. When I finally returned to the West Coast again, we visited and talked on the phone nearly every day. In fact, I believe I was the last one to talk with her on the phone before she died the next day, and I still missed her terribly.

I nervously picked up the receiver, hoping no other family member or friend passed away.

"Hello?"

"Hello, Barb! Did I wake you up?"

"No, I just finished typing a research paper," I said.

I heard my friend's voice on the other end so clearly that it sounded like she was in the next room.

Did you ever receive a phone call, and you immediately recognized the caller's voice, but you just could not place the caller's name? In that case, you don't want to sound stupid or offend the caller by asking, "Who is this?" No, instead you decide to just continue talking with the caller because you will know who the caller is for sure in just a few minutes.

Well, that was the case for me. This caller sounded like my friend Joy, but I immediately dismissed that thought because she had passed away a couple weeks earlier and, of course, dead people do not make phone calls.

"Oh, good!" my caller said. "Then you're still in college?"

"Yes," I said, but all my close friends, neighbors, and

family members already knew that, so my mind was still trying to place who this caller could be.

"Is everything all right?"

"Yeah, I'm fine ... I'm doing fine. Why?"

"I just could not rest until I knew you were okay. I've been so worried about you since you told me that your husband's girlfriend broke up with him. I thought he'd want to come back to you, and I know he'd only end up hurting you again. He'll never change, especially since he ran off with another woman once before and this is the second time. I just don't want you to get hurt again."

"No, you do not have to worry about that," I said. "I'm not taking him back this time. Too much has ... Hello ...Are you still there?"

That's strange, I thought. Suddenly, in the middle of my sentence, I heard a dial tone but no click. I definitely did not hear a click, so I know the caller did not hang up on me.

Because the caller sounded like she was in the next room, I thought it had to be my elderly friend Erma next door. But if it was her, I started to wonder if she was okay because she did not hang up. It was more like the caller just dropped the receiver ... leaving a dial tone but no click.

When this happened in 1981 most phones did not have caller ID, so I could not find out who it was that way. Caller ID was only invented in the 1970s and was not introduced to landline telephones until the late 1980s.

After thinking about it for a few minutes, I decided to call Erma. Her phone must have been on the hook because it was ringing.

"Hello!" her son Pete answered.

"Hi, Pete! This is Barb next door. I hope I did not wake you up, but your mom called me, and I'm worried about her because we suddenly got cut off. She did not hang up but there was just a dial tone like she just dropped the receiver. Would you please check to see if she's alright?"

A few minutes later, Pete returned to the phone.

"Barb, I just checked, and my mom is sleeping. Are you sure she called you?"

"Yes, I'm quite sure … It must have been her … who else could have … "

Pete cut in.

"Here, you can talk to my mom. She's awake now."

"Barb, what's the matter?"

"Well, didn't you just phone me a few minutes ago?"

"No, I was sleeping."

"Oh, I'm sorry I woke you up. I thought it had to be you. It was a familiar voice, and she sounded so close. It was someone who knows me … someone I talk with nearly every day. I know I'm tired right now, but not so tired I imagined it. I just don't know who else it could have been."

"Well, maybe you'll figure out who it was tomorrow," Erma said.

The next day, I asked all of my friends and family members I could think of, and everyone said, "No, it wasn't me. I didn't call you." I even phoned my sister, Pat, long distance because she was the sibling I talked with most often.

"No, it wasn't me either," she said.

I especially did not think it could be her because the caller's voice sounded so close—almost like she was talking from my extension phone.

"That's strange, but I wouldn't worry about it," Pat said.

"Yeah, you're right. It's just such a mystery," I said.

"I received your letter about your friend Joy who recently passed away. How old was she?"

"Joy was only 57," I said. "Joy had to have one of her legs amputated a few years ago. She had diabetes and got an infection in one of her toes that started going up her leg. Because of her diabetes, her doctor said the only way they could stop her infection was to amputate. Joy told me she would rather die than to lose her other leg, too, so maybe it was for the better."

"Oh, I'm sorry to hear that," Pat said. "I never met Joy, but she must have been a very nice lady."

"Yes, she was. She was the nicest person I ever met," I said. "She enjoyed helping others, so it was so difficult for her when she needed help from others instead."

A few weeks later, the phone rang at 7:30 p.m. when I was serving dinner to my sons, Shawn, 10, and Ryan, 5.

"Hello, Barb?" The caller sounded like she didn't know for sure if she called the right number.

"Yes, it's me," I said.

"What are you doing?"

"Oh, I'm serving dinner to my boys."

I soon started talking about the mystery caller I had a few weeks earlier.

"A few weeks ago, I got a call from someone at 1:30 a.m. and I still don't know … "

Suddenly, I paused when I realized this was the SAME voice, the SAME caller who called earlier.

"Is this long distance? "I asked

"Long distance … well, I certainly would say so!" she said.

Then I just blurted it out, "Who is this? "

My caller sounded surprised at my question.

"Don't you know?" she asked.

"Well, I know your voice is familiar … I know you sound just like my friend Joy, but Joy passed away so …"

My caller cut in, "Did that scare you?"

"Well, yes it did scare me," I said. "Wouldn't it scare you if you thought a dead person called you?"

"Oh, I'm so sorry, I didn't think of that. I won't call back again then," she said. "I didn't mean to scare you. I just wanted to make sure you were okay. I just couldn't REST until I knew you were okay."

Suddenly, there was a dial tone and no click ... again, just a dial tone and no click!

"Hello! Hello! Are you there?" I asked. But I got no response.

Shawn looked up from the table.

"Mom, are you okay?" he asked. "Your face looks pale, nearly white."

"Yeah," Ryan said. "Mom, your face looks white!"

"Who was that?" Shawn asked.

"That was Joy," I said. "I'm pretty sure that was Joy."

I never again got another call like that. Is it possible for a loved one to make a phone call from beyond the grave? We might never know for sure until we end up there ourselves.

Microphone Dilemma

Me and my son, Ryan. This is what I wore a month later to the District 32 Toastmasters International speech competition, and I had no pockets to hold the battery pack.

THIS TRUE STORY TOOK place on an elevated stage during my first Toastmaster's International Speech Contest at the district level.

Shortly before the speech contest began, the sergeant-at-arms asked me where my pocket was to hold the battery pack. I was not wearing a jacket or sweater, which usually comes with pockets.

It was panic time. I had no pockets. Oh me, oh my. I didn't know what I should do.

"What battery pack?" I asked him. "Nobody told me I needed a pocket to hold a battery pack!"

Luckily, the sergeant-at-arms was a cool, calm, collected fellow, and he assured me that we would find a workable solution. Then he suggested that I put the battery pack behind the waistband of my skirt, but it had no clip to hold it in place. Worse yet, I happened to be on a fairly successful diet at the time, so the waistband of my skirt was not very snug. So, I put the battery pack inside the elastic band of my panties as well to hold it in place a little better.

Now picture this: It was my first district-level competition, and I had no lectern to hide behind, so that made me nervous enough. To make matters worse, I glanced over to my left and noticed the gentleman I had recently broke up with sat at the same table right next to the new gentleman I just started dating, and that really made me nervous. No young lady wants their previous date to meet their new date. That's never a good thing. But this was no time to allow myself to worry about that.

I had a speech contest to win, so I had to put my love life on hold.

My speech was called "The Forbidden Rock," featuring the story I shared earlier in this book about the time my mother fell into an old abandoned well and was rescued by four of her young children. I started my speech by setting the scene:

The year was 1951, and we lived on a secluded farm in Braham, Minnesota, with woods on two sides. Our nearest neighbor lived about two miles away, and we had no telephone. We were dependent on our windmill to generate enough power for lights and running water in our house. When the wind stopped blowing, my mother lit beeswax candles ....

At that point, I reached for the beeswax candle and matches I brought as props because speakers could get extra points for good visual aids. My biggest concern was that my match may not light on the first strike, but it did, and my speech was off to a flawless start.

As I walked around on stage, however, I could feel the battery pack slightly work its way down. I was really worried about that because a speech like the one I was giving required a lot of hand gestures and body movement. With all that on my mind, it was not easy to block all that out so I could only focus on the words of my speech.

When I got to the most critical part, I had to lean forward.

"Suddenly she slipped, and I heard her scream. My mother fell headfirst into the well ..."

That's when the most terrible thing happened ... zoom, kerplunk! Down went the battery pack into my panties. I looked up with a most horrified look on my face. Of course, I was supposed to have a horrified look on my face because in my story, my mother had just fallen into the well.

I could see that I had the 100-plus audience members on the edge of their seats, and they wanted to know what happened next ... and so did I because I could not remember my next line. I was temporarily speechless. All I could think about was how in the world I would be able to get the battery pack out of my panties up on this elevated stage with no lectern to hide behind in front of all of these people.

After a long silence, I somehow managed to recover and finish my speech. However, I felt sure that even Darren La-Croix, the world champion speaker who gave his winning speech about staying down too long, would think I stayed down too long.

At the end of my speech, I thought about asking my audience to please close their eyes to give me a few moments of privacy, but I felt certain somebody would peek, so I did the next best thing.

I turned around and slowly pulled up on the wire while silently praying that the battery pack would still be attached to the other end. Luckily, it was.

To this day, I don't think the following speaker has any idea the battery pack that was in his pocket had just spent half a speech in my panties. Furthermore, if the sergeant-at-arms knew what happened, he'd probably wear protective gloves for sanitary purposes.

That's how I learned that being prepared means more than just your speech. The lesson I learned was: Don't forget your pockets! Speakers should always wear a sweater or blazer with pockets. But I learned another lesson as well: Life is full of adversities, so we need to learn how to bounce back in the face of any adversity. Show me any successful professional, and I'll show you a person who has learned how to quickly recover from adversity.

The Power of Prayers

IF YOU ARE NOT a religious believer, you probably do not believe there is power in prayers but the older I get the more I believe there is a lot more power in prayers than most of us realize.

My mother definitely believed strongly in the power in prayers. She never failed to get on her knees and pray every morning and night.

When I was a kid, I didn't think about the significance of my mother's prayers, but I think a lot about it now. She did not just say quick little prayers either. When she got on her knees to pray, she prayed for a really long time, and she was still getting on her knees to pray when she was in her 90s in the nursing home. She told me that the nurses would often come and check on her to see if she was still alive because she would be on her knees praying for so long.

If I were in my mother's situation with more than a dozen children, pregnant most of the time and married to an abusive spouse, I doubt I would have had the time, energy, or stamina to be as consistently dedicated to a prayer life as my mother. Looking back now, I think that many times she must have felt too tired or too sick but she never gave herself an excuse not to pray. Regardless of what was happening or how she felt, she always found the time and the strength to say her prayers.

When I got older, I asked my mother what she prayed about, and she said she prayed for the health and safety of all of us kids every day. I pondered over her response for a while because often my mother did not have the strength or courage to protect me and my brothers and sisters from our father's abuse. Instead, she turned us all over to the Lord in prayer.

No angels ever swooped down to grab a switch, board, or

belt away from our Pa when he was beating us, but I guess our mother had great faith that the power of her daily prayers would protect us enough to survive.

After I left the farm and went out into the world on my own, my mother continued to pray. Now I wonder if it was because of the power of her prayers that I'm still alive today. Looking back, I remember at least three times since I left the farm that I came within split seconds of possibly getting killed—but didn't. Could the power of my mother's prayers have made the difference? Perhaps I'll never know for sure, but I'm glad she was a woman of prayer. This is what could have happened when I came within seconds of getting killed.

I was an inexperienced driver. I just got my learner's permit, and my husband decided to give me some driving practice when we were on our way back to Norfolk, Virginia, after visiting Williamsburg. Our first-born son, Shawn, was a baby in his baby chair in the backseat. My husband told me I needed to slow down because I had a lead foot, and I was breaking the speed limit. So instead of looking at the road, I focused my attention on the speedometer, watching for it to go down to 60 mph. As soon as the speedometer got down to 60 mph, I looked up, and it was not a second too soon.

The road ahead was curving over a bridge, and if I had not looked up when I did, our car would most likely have gone over the bridge and fallen into the water far below. Luckily, I reacted quickly enough to make the turn and stay on the road in my lane. My husband was too scared to speak. After that, I never glued my eyes to the speedometer again. I learned from that experience that it's far more important to keep my eyes on the road. Going a little over the speed limit is not nearly as dangerous as flying off a bridge into the water below.

What made the speedometer get down to the right speed limit just in time for me to look up and prevent from driving off the bridge? Did my mother's prayers make the difference? I will never know.

The second time I know I came within seconds of getting killed, my first husband, who was in the Navy at the time, me, and Shawn were moving from Norfolk, Virginia, to Bath, Maine. We were poor and could not afford to stop and spend the night in a motel, so we were taking turns driving straight through more than 800 miles.

I was driving late at night, and it was pitch dark. I had never before seen a tandem gravel truck: the kind with a long, heavy steel arm attached behind it pulling a huge trailer. Because the traffic was getting heavy and our exit was coming up, I needed to pull into the far right lane, so I turned my blinker on and started looking for my opportunity to pull over. When a tandem truck passed me, I was about to pull over behind him as soon as he passed. Because it was so dark, I could not see that long extended arm pulling the heavy trailer behind. I wasn't looking for it either because I was not yet familiar with those trucks. Just as I was ready to pull over, I hesitated just long enough to see the rest of the truck's attachments whiz by. Had I not hesitated those few seconds and pulled in directly behind the first part of that truck, I'm sure we would have been in a horrible accident. Our small Chevy Nova would not have stood a chance against a monster truck like that. Most likely, all three of us would have been killed. That was a hard way to learn about those tandem trucks and what they pull behind them. Ever since then, I always look out for those trucks.

What made me hesitate a few seconds that prevented us from getting into a horrible accident? Did my mother's prayers make the difference? Again, I will never know for sure.

The third time I came within seconds of getting killed happened shortly after I became a single mother. My sons Shawn and Ryan were both in the car with me. It was late at night when we were going to the grocery store. At that time, the first main road, C Street, coming off of 142nd Street where I live seldom got much traffic at all. Of course, I always stopped at the stop sign and looked both ways before pulling out onto C Street. That street got very little traffic, so after looking both ways and seeing it was clear to make my left turn, I always had a habit of pulling all the way over into the far right lane.

Again, it was dark, so I had my headlights on. After looking both ways, I saw no traffic coming I pulled out, but this time, for some unexplained reason, I broke with my habit of pulling all the way over to the right lane and I pulled into the middle turn lane instead. Just as I made my turn, a car with no headlights came out of nowhere and whizzed by in my right-hand lane at about 80 mph. If I had pulled all the way over into that far-right lane, like I always did before, we would surely have been hit, and with the speed that other car was going, we most likely would have all been killed.

To this day, I don't know what made me turn into that middle turn lane instead. Did my mother's prayers make the difference? I might never know for sure, but one thing I do know for sure is that I'm grateful my mother was a woman who believed in the power of prayer.

After my mother passed away at age 93 and was no longer here to pray for the safety of all of her children, most of us started to become a little more cautious. Perhaps my mother's prayers did help keep all 12 of us alive, now ages 62 to 81.

But I wonder what's keeping us alive now? I asked my oldest brother that question.

"Oh, I think Ma is still praying for us," he said.

Missed Opportunities

It's never too late to learn how to paint. This was my first effort in 1975.

It's never too late to learn how to play a musical instrument. This is me with my guitar after I took some lessons at age 20.

"NEVER PUT OFF UNTIL tomorrow what you can do today." Perhaps we should all live by Benjamin Franklin's quote because there might never be a tomorrow. All we have is today – this very day and this very minute – so we cannot count on doing anything tomorrow that we don't do today. Unfortunately, I failed to follow this important advice until I lived to regret it. Some missed opportunities we can get back later on, but some come along once, and only once, in our life time. If we fail to grab it when we have it, all we have left in our head is a great missed opportunity that we will never get again. It's those once-in-a-life-time missed opportunities that will haunt us the most.

MISSED MUSICAL OPPORTUNITY

One of my first missed opportunities was when I wanted to play an instrument in my school band. This one was out of my control. I was only in sixth grade and it cost money for an instrument. My parents received a letter from the school band instructor saying I was the only student in my sixth grade class who received 100 percent perfect score in the test we took to see if we had what it takes to successfully play an instrument in the band. Because of my perfect score, I could have selected any instrument I wanted to play. But I didn't have the money to pay for an instrument and my Pa said maybe he could pay for an instrument the next year. However, I knew the next year would never happen because everyone else started in sixth grade, not seventh. I was right. The next year never happened, so this became my first missed opportunity – never knowing how well I might have done by playing in the band. No student should be denied that opportunity because they cannot afford to pay for a band instrument.

My parents did allow my oldest brother and sister to take private accordion lessons, but they did not even want to learn how to play. None of the rest of us ever got to take lessons. I don't know about the others, but if I had the opportunity to learn how to play the accordion I would most likely still be playing an accordion today.

As soon as I was on my own, however, I bought a Harmony electric guitar, took guitar lessons and was actually learning how to play. Unfortunately, I had to sell my guitar to get enough money to buy food for my sons when I went through an unexpected divorce, but that's another story.

MISSED GRAPHIC ARTIST OPPORTUNITY

I also remember a missed opportunity that I had to become a graphic artist, but once again this one was out of my control.

When I was 15 a man showed up at our farm house during a Minnesota snow blizzard to recruit me to be a live-in student and attend the Minneapolis School of Arts and Graphic Design.

I entered an art competition I saw in a magazine and my entry received a score of 90. The school's representative said that was very good and they only try to recruit students who show the highest potential to become successful graphic artists.

My Pa was still in the barn milking cows at the time he showed up and the snow blizzard was getting worse all the time, so I didn't think the man should wait for Pa to finish his work in the barn and come back to the house. I was also pretty sure Pa would never allow me to have this opportunity, anyway.

"I'm sorry but my parents have so many kids to support I'm sure my Pa would never pay for me to be a live-in student at your school of arts," I said. I felt so badly about turning that poor fellow away with no sale after he drove more than 100 miles in such nasty weather to recruit me.

That was my second missed opportunity. As a child I already showed I had a lot of potential to become a successful graphic artist and sometimes I think about what my life would have been like if I had been able to pursue and develop my artistic talents at the Minneapolis School of Arts.

I never did take a painting class but it's never too late for me to pursue my oil painting endeavors yet. This is another "missed opportunity" I can still do something about.

After all, Grandma Moses was age 77 when she started painting and she lived to be 101. Now her paintings sell for as much as a million dollars.

GREATEST MISSED OPPORTUNITY

When I was 21 and moved from St. Paul, Minnesota, to Tacoma, Washington, I met a dear friend Joy, who practically adopted me. When I married my first husband, who was in the U.S. Navy, we moved to several naval ports, mostly up and down the East Coast. For the next 11 years, I continued to stay in touch with my West Coast mother. We did not yet have access to computers or email, so we communicated with letters and occasional phone calls. I must have written about one letter a week throughout those 11 years, so that would add up to be about 572 letters. My friend Joy frequently told me she thought my letters were too good to throw away, so she decided to keep them in case I wanted to write a book someday, and she did -- all 572 of them. To her, my letters were like a treasure chest full of everything going on in my life, including cute things my first son said and did when he was a toddler. When my husband got out of the Navy and became a commissioned officer in the Air Force, he got stationed at what used to be McChord Air Force Base (now Joint Base Lewis-McChord), so we found ourselves back in Tacoma, Washington. I was so happy I could visit in person with my West Coast mother again. Sadly, Joy had diabetes, and a short time before that she had gotten an infection that started in her toe. Her doctor said the only way to save her life was to amputate her left leg, so Joy was in a wheelchair, and she seldom got an opportunity to go out. So one afternoon we took Joy to the Point Defiance Zoo with us. My son Shawn, age 10, was wearing his Boy Scouts uniform and my son Ryan, age 5, had his cowboy hat and boots on. They both looked so cute and we had a wonderful, but tiring, day.

After we returned to Joy's house, my one and only window of opportunity came. I blew it because I failed to seize the moment. "Before you go, would you like to take all your letters that I saved with you?" Joy asked. "I can go get them for you right now."

I should have agreed to take my letters right then and there, but I had no idea that would be the only opportunity I would ever have to get them.

After that day, my life was turned upside down. Within a few months my husband left me for another woman. I talked with Joy nearly every day on the phone, but that had been the last time I saw Joy alive. She passed away at the young age of 57. As soon as I got a grip, I called Joy's husband Cliff, who was a postman, to see if I could come and get my letters that she had saved, but it was too late. Cliff and his daughter Megan cleaned out all of Joy's belongings and they had already thrown all my letters in the garbage. I felt devastated. After all of those years that she carefully saved my letters and now they were all gone forever.

Cliff and Megan did not see the same value in my letters like Joy did. I felt so disappointed that they did not call to find out if I wanted them. However, I mostly blamed myself for not taking advantage of the one and only opportunity I had to get them when Joy offered them to me a few months earlier.

That's when I learned that today's window of opportunity often becomes tomorrow's missed opportunity. It can be a huge mistake to take it for granted that we will have plenty of opportunities to do something later on because later might never come. I learned this lesson the hard way and I've berated myself for it many times ever since.

Those letters could have been so helpful when I was writing my first book. I still had my file full of notes that I kept for 50 years, but if I could ever do some time travel, I would want to return to that moment of missed opportunity so I could get my letters back.

It is so important to live fully in the moment—each and every moment in our lives, because that's all we really have. None of us are guaranteed tomorrow, so let's strive to make each and every moment count. I imagine many of my readers can remember some missed opportunities they had at various times in their lives too, and that's truly unfortunate.

When couples have more children than they can properly support, many talents and skills may be forever lost. I once heard a Toastmaster's International World Champion speaker say that the richest place on earth is in the graveyard ... because it's full of people who had hopes and dreams of doing things they never did, so all of those treasures that might have been, but never were, are now buried with them. That message had a powerful impact on me.

I started thinking about my hopes and dreams that I had

not yet pursued or achieved, and then I started taking action to make them happen before it's too late. At least as an adult, I found a way to pursue my writing endeavors. Perhaps after I get three or four books published I might take some art classes and start painting again, too. As long as we are walking and breathing, we cannot allow age to get in the way or become an excuse not to do whatever it is that we are here to accomplish. I've tried to live the kind of life where I would have no missed opportunities or regrets, but that's nearly impossible because some things we just cannot control.

We all want to feel like we have control over our lives but sometimes we don't. For instance, many of us have been told there are only two things we cannot control – death and taxes. Of course, there are other things we cannot control either – like the COVID-19 Pandemic. But it's the things we could have controlled, but didn't, that will bother us the most.

I read that some people die agonizing over everything they did wrong or failed to do. While other people die peacefully with a smile on their faces, knowing that they lived their best lives and are ready to move on and join their loved ones in heaven.

Regardless of how much money and power we have, sooner or later we will all die. We know it, but we seldom, if ever, think about it. When we were young we did not feel like we needed to think about dying for a long time yet. We didn't have to, we didn't want to, so we didn't. Even now that we are older, we still don't. Death is not a pleasant thing to think about unless we look forward to going to heaven to be with the loved ones we have already lost. Nevertheless, it is realistic to think about because we all know that one day it will happen to each and every one of us—just when and how most of us never know.

I had a college professor who asked the class to write our own obituary. He said we should write what we would want our obituary to say about our lives and how we lived. A few students wrote serious ones and some wrote humorous ones but many students just starred off into space and were not able to put a single word down on paper. It was not an easy assignment, but doing so forces us to see our lives in a different light. It is often through losing a loved one that makes us value our own lives a little more. Perhaps then, and only then, we become truly motivated to live the most productive, authentic, full, happy lives possible.

As I get older, material things mean less to me and relationships mean more. Now that I am 75, I am much more aware that I might be running out of time. Even if I were blessed with good health to live to 100, I would have only 25 years left. That's not enough time to get everything done that I would still like to do. I value how I spend the time I have left much more than I did when I was young.

Each and every day is a gift from God. When I wake up alive and well on this side of the ground, I ask myself, "What is the most important thing I need to do today?" By asking myself that question I quickly set my priorities, use my time more wisely and get more done.

Our lives are a journey and sometimes we miss opportunities that we will never be able to get back again. However, we can still pursue and experience many missed opportunities in our senior years. They do not all have to be gone forever.

Real Crazy Job Experiences

This is the kind of typewriter
I used to type mortgage documents.

This is me at work, showing the small family
photo on my desk.

DID YOU EVER GET hired twice and fired twice in one hour? I did, and I'm proud of it because that might be a world record. In fact, I should probably be listed in the *Guinness Book of World Records* for being hired and fired the most times in one hour.

No kidding! I will tell you how I managed to make that happen, but first I will give you a little background information to paint a clear picture for younger readers.

When my generation graduated from high school in the mid-1960s, there were no free rides. No "free money" was available from the state or federal government, and nobody that I knew of was allowed to stay home and have Mommy and Daddy support them until they were 30 or 40 years old.

Once my generation turned 18, we were expected to leave home to join the military or get a job to support ourselves and start a life of our own. In fact, we had to get jobs, or we would go hungry and not have a place to live.

That's why I learned how to type and take Gregg stenography. Those job skills were very much in demand at the time.

Two days after my high school graduation, I left my parent's farm in Glenwood, Minnesota, and went to St. Paul to find my first full-time job. I soon learned that sometimes there were as many as 200 applicants competing for one job opening, and it could be difficult to even get an interview.

Thankfully, a friend gave me a creative job-hunting tip: "Whenever you fill out a job application, try to find a way to make your application stand out from all the rest."

That sounded like a really good idea to me, so every time I filled out an application, I tried to think of how I could do that.

When my application asked for my father's occupation, I wrote down that he was a "Big Deal Farmer." That worked because the very next day I got a call for an interview at Northland Insurance Company.

One of the first things the boss, Ernie Crust, said to me was, "To tell you the truth, the main reason I called you in for an interview is because you wrote down here that your father is a 'Big Deal Farmer,' and I never before heard of that. Could you please explain it to me?"

I smiled and said, "Of course. My father is a farmer, and he thinks it's a big deal, so he's a "Big Deal Farmer."

When Crust heard that he laughed so hard that he farted and almost fell out of his chair.

I learned from that experience that in many situations a little humor can help a lot. I got the job and worked there for two years, until I decided to move to the West Coast to a warmer climate. That's when my real crazy job experiences began.

In 1968, when I was 21, I bought a one-way airline ticket to Tacoma, Washington, because I was not going to put up with another Minnesota winter. The only good thing I ever had to say about those long, icy cold Minnesota winters is that it was like living in a human refrigerator, and that's probably why so many Minnesotans look so young for their age.

I didn't have much money, so I knew I would have to find a job quickly. Because I could type 100 words per minute, I felt confident I could find a job within one or two days.

What I did not know is that shortly before I arrived the Boeing Company had just gone through a major layoff of employees, and therefore, nearly every job that was available in Tacoma was now already taken.

The Tacoma Mall was brand new, and downtown Tacoma was still a hustling and bustling place. I went down one street and up the other street and put in a job application at every business that had a typewriter.

Unfortunately, I only got one call for a job interview. When I showed up for my interview, I was in the waiting room for a very long time. The manager kept poking her head out the door but never called me in.

Finally, she walked over to me and asked, "Are you waiting for your mother?"

"No," I said, "My mother lives in Minnesota. I'm waiting for a job interview."

"Oh, I'm sorry," she said. "You have to be at least 18 years old to apply for a job here."

"That's fine," I said, "because I'm 21."

The lady had a most shocked look on her face. Then looking down at my application in her hand, she asked,

"Are you Barbara?" "Yes, I am," I said.

"Oh, my goodness," she said. "I thought you were about 12."

She invited me in for the job interview and apologized for making me wait so long, but she mostly lectured me on how to dress to make myself look older, and I didn't get the job.

After a few weeks I knew I needed to come up with a better job search plan because I was running out of money. In fact, if my second oldest brother had not sent me $200 before I left Minnesota, I would have already run out of money. It was really nice of Bernie to look out for me like that.

I sure was in a pickle because I only bought a one-way ticket and did not have enough money to fly back to Minnesota, even if I wanted to. So, I had to come up with Plan Number 2.

I asked myself, "What am I not doing and what could I do differently?" That's when I realized I was only applying for all of the jobs I was qualified to do, but I was missing out on all of the other jobs I was not qualified to do. I remembered somebody once told me that if you go to the library and you look up a company and learn some of the jargon the company uses for certain jobs you can apply for a job you're not qualified to perform and get hired, anyway. At that point, I thought that might be a good idea, so I decided to try it.

In desperate times, we might have to do desperate things, right? So, instead of looking for a job I was qualified to do I decided to purposely fake my way into a job I was not qualified to do. I thought by the time they found out I would at least have another paycheck. That might give me enough time to find a job I could keep.

Plan Number 2 worked. I got hired at Pacific Insurance Company to transcribe letters for several different insurance agents using a Dictaphone. It was a popular machine back then and was something like a tape recorder with earphones that was operated with a foot pedal. I could back it up to repeat a word or phrase or make it go faster to keep up to my typing speed.

Each insurance agent had a particular format they wanted me to use when I typed their letters. For example, one wanted me to always use digits for the date; another one wanted me to type the day first, then the month and the year; and a third one wanted me to type the month, the day, and the year. It was difficult to remember what format each one wanted. In short, it was a very demanding, fast-paced, high-pressure job. I gave it my best effort and managed to keep that job a lot longer than I thought I would. I kept wondering why it was taking them so long to figure out that I was not qualified, and I was even beginning to think I might actually be qualified to keep that job.

What finally exposed my lack of qualifications was the day I was transcribing a letter from an insurance agent who had a strong Southern accent and his use of the word "nomenclature." It was difficult enough to understand what this agent was saying when he used common terms, much less a word I never before heard in my life.

I kept rewinding that part on my Dictaphone in an effort to figure out what the heck that agent was saying, but no matter how many times I played it back, it sounded like he was saying "normal nature," even though that did not make any sense, so that's what I finally typed.

When my manager saw that, I was fired on the spot.

Nevertheless, I was proud that I was able to keep that job long enough to get three pay checks, instead of only one. In fact, I was so happy I went out to the Tacoma Roller Bowl to celebrate my huge accomplishment.

The next day, I was job hunting again for a position I could keep for a few years, but I knew my pay checks would not last too long, so then I went to Plan Number 3—an employment agency that I would have to pay to help me find a job. That's where I met my friend Joy Deakes, who worked at the employment agency.

The next day, she sent me to apply for a job at FirstBank Mortgage Company. They needed a good, accurate typist to fill out mortgage papers. I thought that interview went well, and I got the job.

Accuracy was very important in those days because every time a mistake was made, we had to pull out all of the paperwork, put in a new form, and start over again. Liquid white out did not work because each set of mortgage documents had several carbon copies.

My supervisor was very happy with my work because I

seldom made typing errors, and I was pumping out those mortgage papers faster than another girl who was doing the same job for a long time. That's why I was so surprised when my nice supervisor pulled me aside about three weeks later with some unexpected news.

"I want to give you a heads up," she said. "Our manager is an alcoholic, and she was drunk when she hired you. She gets sober about once every three weeks. This morning, she got sober and asked me who you were and where you came from. I reminded her that she hired you three weeks ago. She asked how you were doing, and I told her you were doing really well. Then she said she had one too many employees, so she was going to have to let someone go. Since you were the last one she hired, she said it would have to be you. I know it's not fair, and I feel really bad about that. I just want you to know that she will be calling you in today to let you go." "Thanks for warning me, but don't worry," I said. "When the manager calls me in, at least I will make her feel really bad for letting me go."

"How will you do that?" she asked.

"I'll show her my photo of the large family I come from, and I will tell her that I understand her dilemma of having one person too many, but the worst part is that I'm trying to save enough money to buy my poor mother an automatic washer for Christmas. She still has to wash all her clothes on a scrub board, and sometimes her knuckles bleed."

My supervisor laughed and thought I was just joking until she saw me grab the family photo when the manager called me in. After I told the manager my sob story, it worked better than I thought it would.

"Oh, my goodness," she said. "Now I really feel badly about having to let you go. I'll tell you what, you can go to lunch now, and I will check the other departments to see if we have another job opening. I'll let you know when you get back."

That sounded pretty good, but I was not counting on it. As far as I knew, I would have to find another job, so I asked the waitress at the café where I ordered my egg salad sandwich every day if she knew of any job openings.

"As a matter of fact," she said. "That fellow who was just in here from Richards Commercial Photography Studio told me that they are looking for a Girl Friday to do a variety of office work. They are located just around the corner from here, and if you go over there now, you might be able to get that job because they need somebody right away."

I quickly gobbled up my lunch and ran over to apply for the job. They gave me a typing and spelling test, which I passed with flying colors, so I immediately got an interview with the big boss, Edward Richards himself.

Keep in mind that in those days, bosses could get away with saying and asking pretty much anything. So this is how that interview went:

"According to your typing and spelling test, you are certainly well qualified to do this job," Richards said. "But you are such a pretty young girl, how do I know that you will not get pregnant and run off with some young man in a couple of weeks?"

"That won't happen because I have high moral standards and I'm not that kind of girl," I said. "Besides, I'm not in a hurry to get married because my parents had 14 kids, and I don't want to change more poop diapers or hear more crying babies for a long time."

"Well, what if you date a young man you don't know very well, and he ends up raping you and getting you pregnant?"

"That won't happen either," I said. "If I date a guy I don't know very well, I grease my neck down with Vicks Vapor Rub and if he tries to get fresh, he gets a mouth full of Vicks Vapor Rub and that works every time. I haven't ever been raped yet."

After hearing that, Richards hired me and said I could start on Monday. Now I had a job again.

Then I hurried back to the office where I had just been fired, and as soon as I returned the supervisor told me that the manager was running around like a chicken with its head cut off trying to find another position for me.

To my surprise, the manager at FirstBank Mortgage called me into her office a few minutes later to inform me that she found another position in one of the other departments, so I was hired again. I was dumbfounded, because that meant I had two jobs, and I could only do one full-time job at a time. I didn't know what to do, so I sat down and thought about it for a few minutes. I had to choose which job I would keep. I thought if I kept the FirstBank Mortgage job the manager might get drunk again and forget she hired me back, so I didn't think that job would be very stable. I also knew that if I kept that job, I would have to pay the employment agency that got me the job, but if I lost that job after only three weeks, the employment agency would give me a refund for the $300 fee.

Since I got the job at Richards Commercial Photography Studio on my own, I would not have to pay a fee. So, I went back in to talk to the FirstBank Mortgage manager again.

"I really appreciate that you offered me another job, but during my lunch I found another job at Richard's Commercial Photography Studio," I said. "I found that job on my own, so I would not have to pay the employment agency if

I take that job. If you write a note saying you fired me from this job, I would get a refund for the $300 from the employment agency, and then I could buy my mother that automatic washer even sooner."

"What would you like me to do?" she asked.

"Could you please fire me again," I said. "I need you to write a note to the employment agency so I can get my money back?"

"Sure, just tell me what to say," she said.

That is how I got hired twice and fired twice in one lunch hour.

I worked at Richards Commercial Photography Studio for more than a year, until I moved to San Diego, California.

As for that automatic washer, my mother got an inheritance from her father and she already had one—so shame on me.

Another Life,
Another Time

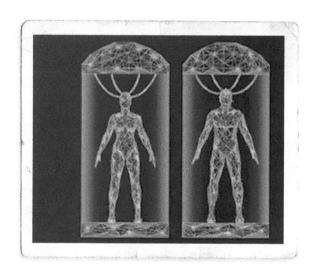

CANCER DOES NOT HAVE any respect for wealth or
fame, and Bill Jetson was no exception. He was dying, and
no doctor in the world could save him. Yet, Jetson could not
accept that his life was coming to an end. He built his entire
fortune by making tough decisions and beating odds, and he
wasn't about to give up now. Jetson believed there had to be
some kind of alternative, some hope, and he was determined
to find it.

During the next few months, Jetson met with top medical
and scientific experts. Finally, he discovered one possibility,
one chance open to him to extend his life, and Jetson decided
to take it.

A few months later, January 5, 2012, at the young age of
46, Jetson died. Immediately upon his death, Jetson's body
was deep frozen in liquid nitrogen. A thin layer of frost cov-
ered his face. His body was wrapped in aluminum foil, and
he was placed in a capsule that looked like a flattened bot-
tle-shaped container. Jetson's body was then placed in an un-
derground storage area near Los Angeles. In other words,
Bill Jetson was put in a state of cryogenic suspension in the
hope that when medical science became more advanced, he
might be brought back to life again. At some distant time in
the future, there was a chance that Jetson could be thawed
from his deep frozen state and cured of the cancerous disease
that took his life.

Fortunately, Jetson's wealth made it possible for him to
make the necessary arrangements for this expensive and un-
usual method of entombment. It cost a whopping $100,000
for him to be put in the state of cryogenic suspension, and it

would cost another \$50,000 a year, thereafter, for storage fees—all which had to be paid for in advance for the next 250 years.

One hundred and eighty-two years later, scientists and medical doctors were busy preparing to bring Jetson back to life. Great strides in medical technology had been perfected, and now all forms of cancer were easy to cure.

The same team of doctors already tried to revive four other bodies that were in cryogenic suspension. The first three attempts were complete failures. The fourth frozen body of Walt Goldman was brought back to life, but the results were tragic. Goldman was deep frozen 30 years prior to Jetson, when cryogenics was still in the infant stages. Consequently, it was impossible to freeze his entire brain and other tissues fast enough to avoid the destruction of vital cells. Therefore, Goldman was brought back to life with severe brain damage and the previously celebrated genius could merely function as half a man.

Nonetheless, the doctors who specialized in cryogenics were very hopeful about the prospects of Bill Jetson. Cryogenics was much more advanced at the time of Jetson's death and complete success was much more promising because he could very well be brought back to life without having any damaged cells whatsoever.

Heading up the team of doctors was a direct descendant of the deep frozen subject, Dr. Preston Jetson, who had a personal interest in the success of this revival.

After 182 years of being in a deep frozen state, enthusiasm soared when Jetson moved, opened his eyes, and asked, "What's for breakfast? I'm starving!"

Not realizing where he had been for the past 182 years, but otherwise alert and intelligible, Jetson was revived and given a second chance at life in another time.

Jetson did not recognize a single familiar thing on his breakfast plate. Nonetheless, he did not hesitate to eat. It wasn't long, however, before he started asking questions.

"What happened? Where am I? How did I get in this hospital? Where is my wife? When can I see her?"

Of course, Dr. Jetson would eventually answer all of his great, great, great, great grandfather's questions, but not just yet. This was another time in history quite different from the previous life that Jetson had known and having this knowledge too soon could cause him to go into severe shock. The first few days of his second life would be very crucial. Therefore, when and how Dr. Jetson would answer his patient's questions was indeed a delicate situation that would have to be handled very carefully.

All the doctors on his team agreed that it would be best if Jetson were not told anything during those first two days. How would he feel when he learned that his former family members and friends lived and died in another century? How would he feel when he discovered his wife passed away 152 years ago, 30 years after he did? The answers to these questions would have to wait, but they would be forthcoming. The first two days Jetson would have to be kept as calm as possible.

The fifth day, Jetson felt well enough to get out of bed. Looking around at the doctors and his assistants, Jetson noticed the unusual uniforms that they were wearing, and he began to wonder why they were dressed like that.

"Do I have a contagious disease?" he asked "Why won't you let me have a newspaper, telephone, or television? What kind of place is this, anyway?"

Jetson wanted to receive answers to his questions now, so

he decided to sneak out of his room and go look for a phone the first chance he got.

Pretending to be in a deep sleep, Jetson was alone in his room at last, so he sat up in bed. He felt a little light-headed at first, but after a few moments his dizziness left, and he felt strong enough to stand. Jetson then tried to walk, but his legs felt like rubber bands disconnected from his joints. They simply would not cooperate, and then his legs gave way and he collapsed to the floor. At least, Jetson was able to pick himself up and get back into bed.

Still, he decided he would try again later whenever no one was around, and he managed to take a couple more steps each day he tried. Slowly Jetson made his way closer and closer to the door in the huge room. Finally, he reached for the knob, but there wasn't any. Instead, the door slid into the wall automatically.

Peeking out of the door, Jetson saw a strangely shaped hallway, and to his astonishment, the floor was moving. He hesitated before carefully stepping onto the moving floor. As he was carried down the winding hallway, Jetson kept looking for a phone because wanted to call his wife to ask her to take him out of this foreign hospital. Finally, Jetson could not find a single phone booth but realized he could not make a call, anyway, because he had no money with him.

However, he saw a room that had something that looked like TV screens so he decided to check that out. Then he saw a sign that read, "To make a call, tap your microchip to the screen."

Jetson wondered where in the world he would be able to get a microchip, so he asked another person in the room.

"Oh, don't you have one in your hand?" the man asked.

Jetson opened his hands and showed the man they were

empty.

"No, I mean you should have one embedded under your skin in your right hand. We all do. It's the law."

Jetson stepped back onto the moving floor in the hallway. Suddenly it came to a stop in front of a huge window, and he couldn't believe what he was seeing. Could it be? Could it really be? Was that a submarine out there or were his eyes deceiving him? Jetson forced himself to look closer. There was dark green and black water everywhere. Then he saw a shark and an octopus. Could it be that this hospital was under water in an ocean?

Suddenly, Dr. Jetson showed up.

"What on earth are you doing out of bed?" he asked.

At least, Dr. Jetson used the word "earth" so he must not have been abducted by aliens and taken to some alien station in the ocean.

"This is not a hospital. It's a laboratory," Dr. Jetson said. "I will take you back to your room, and I will answer your questions now."

When Jetson learned that he was the first person to ever be successfully brought back to a second life, at first he felt like he was the luckiest, most powerful, super human that ever existed. But it wasn't long before he started feeling something else.

When Dr. Jetson told his patient that he was actually his direct descendant, it was pretty difficult for him to comprehend that his doctor was his great grandson times four, but at least when he was ready to leave, he was invited to stay at his distant relative's house. Dr. Jetson wanted to continue to monitor and document him, anyway.

Getting into a large, cylinder shaped elevator, Jetson and his doctor strapped themselves into a bucket seat. Within a few minutes, they were shot to the surface of the water, where Dr. Jetson's "bird" waited to pick them up. His "bird" was a hovering mini jet express vehicle that took the place of cars and was now the main source of transportation above water. Dr. Jetson waived his microchipped hand over a scanner and then sat back and relaxed. Within a few minutes, with no traffic jams or delays, they arrived at Dr. Jetson's solar home and parked.

When Jetson and his distant grandson entered the house, they were greeted by Elsie, the robot maid, who kissed each one on the cheek and hung up their coats. That was the first time Jetson had ever been kissed by a robot, and he hoped it would be the last. The solar house was virtually self-sufficient.

Jetson then walked into the living room where he noticed something that looked like an aquarium. However, what was in the tank looked instead very much like a human baby. Dr. Jetson explained: "What you think you see is correct. We are awaiting the birth of our first child. Pregnancy has been eliminated. What we have now are test-tube babies, which are ordered from a baby bank catalog. We can watch our baby grow until his preselected birth date at which time we will simply remove him from his artificial womb. Then we will return the Embryo Tank to the Baby Bank Center to receive a $5,000 return deposit along with our child's official birth records.

Dr. Jetson continued to explain how it worked. Any man who wants to make a biological donation to the baby bank can fill out an application to do so, but only those shown to have specific hereditary backgrounds are selected for their services for a period of five years, and they are most highly compensated. The staff at the Baby Bank Center matches the most compatible subjects to obtain the desired results, thereby eliminating all birth defects. As soon as conception has taken place, the embryo is placed into the artificial womb and listed in the baby catalog.

Married couples who want to have children can now choose the gender, hair color, eye color, and other physical features that are most appealing to them. However, all couples are limited to a maximum of three children. Couples who earn below the median wage bracket are not allowed to order children.

The thought of test-tube babies made Jetson feel chilly, and he broke out in goose bumps. Putting his hand to his cheek, he tried to warm the cold spot where Elsie the robot kissed him.

Jetson felt himself living in a world in which he did not and probably never would, belong. He was a grown man who was seeing and learning about his environment as though he were a baby himself. This way of living seemed so impersonal, mechanical, and fast. The clothes, food, and travel were all different, and there did not appear to be anything left that could make Jetson feel like he was at home. He saw himself in the news as the star of a freak show. He might just as well have been taken prisoner and sent to another planet.

Now Jetson knew that his quest for a second life was all a bad mistake. He would never be able to enjoy or even cope with this kind of life.

The next morning, Jetson awoke to the sound of an alarm. Lying next to him was his wife. He found himself in his own home, in his own time. Jetson took a deep breath in a sigh of relief. Then he reached for the phone before it was too late. "I want to cancel those arrangements we made yesterday," he said.

Realizing that in reality he was still a dying man, Jetson was now ready to accept his fate. His vivid dream made him understand something he had previously refused to consider. Living another life in another time would be a far greater struggle and much more difficult to face than death itself. He would draw the line and die gracefully.

Mrs. Whatchamacallit

AUTHOR'S NOTE

My "guest writer" is my former husband (Ret.) Lt. Col. Donald R. Sellers, who wrote the last short story in my book, "Mrs. Whatchamacallit."

When Don and I were married, he volunteered to help me edit the Army newspaper, The Northwest Guardian, and then he decided to become a writer himself. At first, I did not know if it were possible for someone to just decide to become a professional writer so late in life, but Don proved he could do it. So far, Don wrote 16 short stories, 9 flash fiction, and 16 commentaries. He has always been a book lover and avid reader and I'm sure that helped.

"Mrs. Whatchamacallit" is still my favorite. When Don wrote that story, he asked for my feedback. After the first couple revisions, I said his organization and descriptions were great, but it lacked the emotional pull that tugs on a reader's heart strings. Finally, when Don's story brought tears to my eyes, I knew that he nailed it.

Don entered this story in the extremely competitive World Wide Writers short story contest, and he won third place and $200.00. Since then, Don has revised it again. I love this story, and I think it deserves to be shared with more readers, so I asked Don to give me permission to include his story in my book for your reading pleasure.

Don is 87 and he still uses his leadership skills and remains active in life. He now serves as the president of our Toastmaster's International Club 1123, and he also serves as the leader of the Plateau Area Writer's Association.

MY DAD SAYS WE LIVE in small-town America. "Jimmy boy," he told me, "Plum Lake, Wisconsin, is the best kept secret in the good ole U.S. of A ... neat, clean, and free of riffraff. Be glad you're an Olson."

He must be right. When I ride my bike down the alleys and look at the backyards on both sides of me, everything looks really neat. I help my dad a lot in the backyard: mow the grass, pull weeds, and put the trash out on Thursday mornings for the garbage man. We take good care of our back porch, too. Mom sweeps it every day and has flowers in some boxes along the sides. I park my bike on the back porch at night, and I don't even have to lock it up.

All of the backyards in this neighborhood look really neat—well almost. Down in the next block, there was a trashy house. The backyard was really messy. Nobody ever mowed the grass or pulled weeds, and on the back porch sat an old washer with a ringer and a tub for rinsing clothes. Yes, sir, my dad said, that back porch needed a lot of work. It needed painting and someone to just clean up the mess.

Mrs. Whatchamacallit lived there. We called her Mrs. Whatchamacallit because her name was too long and too hard to say. It began with the letters G-r-b-z- and kept right on going for 11 more letters and ended in the letter I. Can you imagine that? Fifteen letters in the last name and only two vowels.

One Saturday afternoon, I saw Mrs. Whatchamacallit standing on the back porch looking at the washing machine. I stopped my bicycle and watched her. It was the first time I had seen her. She looked just like the witch in *The Wizard of Oz,* only she didn't have the black, pointy hat. Would you believe it? She leaned on a cane and wore a heavy black dress that went all the way to the ground with a black shawl around her neck. She must never have combed her hair. It was snowy white and ran in strings to her shoulders. She sure must have been hot and sweaty. It was July, and the sun made my bicycle feel hot.

She saw me there on my bike with one foot on the ground and the other on the pedal. When I saw her looking at me, I got ready to leave.

Then she said, "Sonny, could you help me?"

At least, I think that's what she said. I had a hard time understanding her, 'cause she sounded just like the witch in *The Wizard of Oz, too.* What was it my mother said? "Witches cackle."

"Sonny, I really need some help. Could you get off your bicycle and come over here and help me?"

Again, I think that's what she said. The words didn't come out like good English. I was only 10 years old then, and I was scared—really scared. But I decided to help her anyway. I kicked the kick stand on my bike, left it standing on the gravel in the alley, and walked to the porch.

As I got closer I noticed that she smelled, and her teeth were yellow and looked like they needed brushing.

"Sonny, I have some clothes in my bedroom. Could you carry them to the washing machine for me?"

That's not the way she talked, but it's what she meant. She limped along on her cane, and I followed her into the house. The kitchen was sort of messy, with cooking pots, dishes, and flour and spices all over. Everything in the rest of the house was neat, but all the window shades were pulled tight.

It smelled old inside, except for the kitchen. The kitchen smelled strange, like nothing I had never had a whiff of before. I could tell it had something to do with her cooking. But I wasn't sure I wanted to eat anything in there.

I carried the basket full of sheets and clothes to the back porch.

"I can put these in the washing machine if you like," I said.

"Sure, Sonny, that will help. Do you have a name?"

"My dad calls me Jimmy Boy."

"That's a fine name. Can I call you Jimmy Boy?"

"I guess so. What's your name?"

She told me. I couldn't pronounce it, no matter how much I tried, so I asked her to spell it for me. She went inside and wrote it down on a piece of paper.

I took it home and showed my dad. He looked at the paper and said, "Damn foreigners. I can't make heads or tails of this name. She must be a Polack, or from Czechoslovakia or from someplace in the Balkans. Jimmy Boy, just call her Mrs. Whatchamacallit. That's good enough. What are you doing over there anyway?"

I told my dad how I helped Mrs. Whatchamacallit with her washing. He allowed that was all right. But he said, "Be careful now, Jimmy Boy, you never know what a Polack might do."

I asked my dad to write out the name Mrs. Whatchamacallit for me. He took a pencil and wrote it out on a piece of paper.

I took the name back to Mrs. Whatchamacallit, showed it to her, and asked her if it was all right to call her Mrs. Whatchamacallit.

She looked at the piece of paper and said, "Jimmy Boy, I think this name is almost as long as my real name. Let's count the letters."

Together, we counted fifteen letters.

"Jimmy Boy," she said, "this name has as many letters as

my own name." She leaned forward and smiled at me, "Of course, it's all right to use this name. But I do have a first name. It is Marja. Can you say that?"

I could say that. I said it several times so she could see that I could say it.

"That's fine, Jimmy Boy," she said. "You may call me Marja, if you like. I like that name. But if you ever can say my last name, would you say it for me?"

I discovered that Mrs. Whatchamacallit was lots of fun. I went over there regular-like, almost every day now, even when school started. We got to be good friends, and I could even understand her now when she talked. She didn't even look so bad anymore, and she didn't smell either.

I helped her with things that were hard for her to do, like the washing and putting her groceries away. Once a week on Wednesdays, she would call in her order, and the delivery man from Red Owl would bring groceries to the front door. I would carry the sacks to the kitchen, and she would show me where to put everything.

She even let me sweep the kitchen floor and straighten the mess on the porch. I asked her if I could pull the shades and open the windows. She allowed that was okay. I figured she didn't do these things because she didn't walk very well. I pulled weeds around the house and asked my dad if I could borrow the lawn mower to mow the lawn.

"Why are you doing all this?" my dad asked.

I told him this was my good-deed task for Boy Scouts. I didn't tell him I liked Mrs. Whatchamacallit, and I liked doing things for her. It didn't seem right to tell him that.

Mrs. Whatchamacallit liked to talk a lot. She would talk from the time I got there until the time I left. I guess she was lonely. Nobody ever came to see her but me.

One day I asked her if she was Polack. She straightened herself as much as she could and said, "I am Polish, and I was born in the old country—Poland. So was my husband."

"Is that the same as Polack?"

She put her hand softly on my head and looked me straight in the eye, "It is, Jimmy Boy, it is. But Polish is so much nicer. Don't you ever forget that."

I thought it strange that she always wore black clothes, so one day I asked her why she didn't have clothes of different colors.

She went to the bedroom and came back with a book of photographs. "Jimmy Boy, these are pictures of the old country and of me and my husband in New York. His name was Jan. Do you like that name?"

I allowed that I did. I repeated it several times for her, saying Jan Whatchamacallit. "Marja, those two names really go good together," I said.

She laughed really hard.

She told me she came over here in 1946 after the big war. She and her husband lost their families: their aunts, uncles, cousins, and most of their friends during and after the war. They were all killed by the Nazis and the communists. She and Jan sneaked out of Poland and came to New York to start a new life. The last thing she remembered was soldiers burning her house.

I knew about war. Sometimes my friends and I would play war and pretend to kill each other. We thought it was fun to pretend to be killed and fall down dead. Somehow, now, I no longer feel good about playing war. Maybe I would never play war again.

"It was hard for Jan to find work in New York," she said one day. "All of the good jobs went to Americans coming back from the war. He took a job with the Mafia, as a bag man for the numbers racket."

I didn't understand that, so I asked her about it. She explained it to me, and said it was wrong and that Jan would go to jail if the police caught him.

That didn't sound right to me. The way she explained it, someone always won a big prize of money, and I figured that was all right.

"They killed my husband," she said. "He told me to take money from our bank and go west if anything happened to him. So, I buried him and took the train until I came to a town I liked.

"Yes, Jimmy Boy, I do have other clothes. But I wear black because I love my husband. I loved him so much I will wear these clothes until I die. You might not understand this. I honor my husband with my clothing."

I remember her talking these words. While I didn't understand them then, I thought that someday I would.

"So, Jimmy Boy," she said. "Here I am. I came here 15 years ago. That was before you were born."

One time I asked her if she had a little boy or girl of her own. She said she had a little boy who was killed in Poland. She and her husband wanted children when they came to New York. But no matter how much they wanted or how much they tried, they never got any more children. She asked me if I would be her little boy, if my mother and father would share me with her.

I said I would ask. I never did. I thought that Mom and Dad would be upset if I asked—especially Dad. So, the next day, I came back and told her it was all right for me to be her little boy.

She gave me a great big hug. I guess she thought it was

okay now to give me hugs.

I hugged her back.

I especially liked to be there when she was cooking. She made good things. She was a good cook—maybe even better than my mom. The kitchen really smelled good now, and it no longer looked messy to me, although it was. She never let me straighten the kitchen. She said she knew where everything was, and if I moved things, she wouldn't be able to cook.

She made all kinds of good things—cakes, cookies, and breads. She gave them all strange names, most of which I can't remember now, except for babka. It was a cake with fruit in it. She said it was like our pound cake.

She made something called polenta from cornmeal. She said it was not really Polish food, but she and Jan liked it. They learned to eat it during the war. It was really good when she put jam on it.

One day she asked me if I would like to ask my mom and dad over for dinner.

"Wow," I said. "That's a good idea."

"I can make some cabbage soup, potatoes, chicken, and dumplings. I make a really good goulash with polish sausage that your mom and dad will like. It was Jan's favorite dish. Then for dessert, we will have some babka."

"Oh boy, as soon as my dad comes home from work, I will ask him and my mom."

And so, I did. I asked my mom and dad that evening at the supper table. Mom really liked the idea. But my dad said, "Go over to that old fart's house? Not only no, but hell no. None of that foreign crap for me. Cabbage soup, ugh!" He got up from the table and left the kitchen holding his nose. Then he put his head back through the door and asked, "Jimmy Boy, when will you finish up with that Boy Scout project?"

I went back the next day and told Mrs. Whatchamacallit that my mom and dad were too busy to come and eat supper at her house.

She said, "I understand, Jimmy Boy. Someday, if your mother and father will let you, perhaps, you and I can have dinner here."

〜〜〜

One Thursday, during the summer when I was 11, the delivery man from Red Owl came to our front door. "Does Jimmy Olson live here?"

My mom called me to the front door.

"Jimmy," he said, "I'm John. You should know me. I deliver groceries for the Red Owl."

I nodded my head, wondering why he came to our front door.

"Mrs. ----------,"

He said the name I couldn't say.

"... didn't call in her order on Wednesday, and we thought maybe something happened. So, I went over to her house and knocked on the front door. Nobody answered, and we're worried. I see you over there a lot. Do you know where she is? Is she all right?"

Marja was dead. I knew she had died as surely as I was standing at the front door. I really felt badly. I had not been over there since Monday.

"She always leaves the back door open," I told the delivery man. "I'll meet you there." I got my bike off the back porch and beat the delivery man to Marja's house. When he got there, he said, "Let me go in first."

I followed him into the kitchen. He looked in the living room and asked, "Where's the bedroom?" I pointed to a closed door.

I went back into the kitchen and stood. I felt strange. The kitchen felt strange. I knew I would never see Marja cook again. I would never see those hands fly fast, those hands that knew where everything was. It was almost like magic. She would put things in the oven, and out they would come smelling and tasting good. I knew that I had missed the best thing of all. I would never get to taste her really good goulash again.

"She's dead, Jimmy. She's dead," the delivery man called out to me.

"I know," I said. "I know."

I bolted for the door to the living room.

John grabbed me as I ran by. "Better not go in there, Jimmy, it's pretty ripe." He held me tightly by the hand. "I want you to get on your bicycle and go home for now. Can you get home okay?"

I nodded.

"I'll call the police and get an ambulance over here," he said. "Jimmy, I'll come over and talk to you later. Okay."

I got on my bike and went home and upstairs to my bed and cried. I know boys aren't supposed to cry. But I cried anyway.

Mom came up later, and I told her what happened. She just held me. I could see tears in her eyes.

Later that evening, John came over and told me that Mrs. Whatchamacallit died of a heart attack. He said that the body was at the Adams Funeral Home. I could go see it tomorrow.

A priest came by. He said Mrs. Whatchamacallit was Catholic and in his parish. He wanted to talk with me, and so we did. We talked for a long time, and I told him about Marja and me. He told me they would put a headstone on her grave. He asked: Did I want to put something on the headstone. I thought for a little while and told him what I wanted to say. He said that was good.

Then he asked me if he could put something on the headstone. I allowed that it was all right. He told me what he was going to say. I said it was good.

My mom took me to the funeral home the next night. Mrs. Whatchamacallit lay in a coffin with her black dress and black shawl. It looked like her, and yet, it didn't look like her. Something was missing. She looked like the statues I see on TV or in my school books.

I knew I would never hear her say "Hi, Jimmy Boy" again, or look with her at scrapbooks again, or hear her say, "Jimmy Boy, I need some help with the washing."

I stood there looking at her, I wanted to say something, but the words wouldn't come. Mom and I and the priest were the only ones who came to visit her and go to the funeral.

A few days later, my mom said we all have to go see a lawyer.

"What for?" I asked.

She said he was going to read the will of Mrs. Whatchamacallit.

"What was a will?" I asked.

She said sometimes people make a will before they die, and they leave money and things to other people.

So, we went to this big office with lots of carpets and soft chairs and listened to the lawyer. He said Mrs. Whatchamacallit left me all her money—about $40,000. My mother started crying.

But my dad stood up and walked back and forth saying,

"Well, I'll be damned. I knew the old bitch had some money."

The lawyer said I was supposed to use this money to go to college, and if anything was left over, I would get it when I got to be 30 years old. But I would have to be a good citizen.

I know that $40,000 is a lot of money, but I think I would rather have Marja.

They burned Marja's house. John came over and told me they were going to do it. I went over to watch. One of the firemen said this was practice, so that when they had a real fire they could put it out quickly. While I watched the house burning, all I could think of was that this was the second time they burned Marja's house. I didn't understand it.

Mom and dad talked about the firemen burning the house.

My dad said, "It was good riddance. Anyway, someone had already bought the property and was going to build on it."

"It feels like genocide," my mom said. "It's as if we were trying to rid the town of her memory."

I wasn't quite sure what genocide meant. But I thought if it meant what I thought, getting rid of people who are different, I don't like it. It doesn't matter, I'll always remember Mrs. Whatchamacallit.

Right after the funeral, I went to see Marja's grave every day. I would pick wildflowers along the way and place them on her grave. Sometimes, it would be dandelions. Then, I would read the headstone.

First, there was her real name.

Then my words: Mrs. Whatchamacallit was a fine Polish lady.

Then the words from the priest: She went to heaven with honor.

I don't go every day anymore, but I still go a lot. My

mother says fall is coming. There won't be flowers to pick.

I remember seeing a story on TV about a man whose friend died. He would go to her grave and throw himself on top with his stomach down and his arms and legs spread out. He said he could hear her. They could talk together.

I think I'll do that today. Maybe Marja and I can talk. I want to tell her that someday, when I can say her real name, I will come and say it for her.

Sometimes, bringing flowers just doesn't seem to be enough.

The End

ACKNOWLEDGMENTS

Special thanks to all of my dear friends over the past 25 years who were always there for me through good times and bad: Carole Kaye Davis, Patricia Palmer, Sally Drexler, Margarete Campbell, April Anderson, Billie Stewart, Tobias Stewart, Veronica Baker, Mandy Stocker, and Lyndah Wallin and my great neighbors Josie and Joe Crespin and Paul and Kirstin Courtney.

You all have done something that made my life better in one way or another, and I appreciate you very much. No one could ever ask for better, more thoughtful friends and neighbors.

May God bless you all!

MY BEST MENTORS

I dedicated this book to my four best mentors, who significantly encouraged me in my writing endeavors, but I would like my readers to know a little more about them.

When I was nine years old, I wrote letters to my maternal grandmother, Marion Harrison Brewster. She was the first person to recognize that I was a gifted writer. Grandma Brewster lived in Warroad, Minnesota, which was 281 miles from our farm in Glenwood, Minnesota, so family gatherings with Grandma Brewster were rare. When we took the four-hour, 51-minute road trip, however, Grandma always made me feel special.

I remember one Thanksgiving when everyone was gathered around a huge, long table and Grandma stood at one end and tapped her glass to get everyone's attention. "Before we begin eating," she said, "I just have to read a letter I received from Barbara." As Grandma read my letter, everyone laughed and applauded. By reading my letter, Grandma Brewster recognized me for something I could do well that set me apart from my many brothers and sisters. In other words, my gift for writing was something that made me stand out in the crowd. Some of my other siblings are also excellent writers, but none of them were really interested in writing at a young age, so I had no competition.

Sadly, I lost my Grandma Brewster when I was only 14 because she died from a brain aneurism at just 60 years old. However, she profoundly influenced my career path. I wish Grandma Brewster would have lived long enough to know how her encouraging, supportive words helped put me on a path toward a successful writing career.

My seventh-grade English teacher, Betty Bradfield, made learning English grammar so much fun that I always looked forward to her classes. For example, she gave us assignments where we were allowed to write our own sentences and then put one line under the subject and two lines under the verb. Later we had similar assignments to recognize adverbs, adjectives, prepositions, and prepositional phrases. During her classes, Bradfield asked students to volunteer to come up to the front of the classroom and write our sentences on the chalk board. I always volunteered because I wrote such creative and funny sentences that it made my classmates laugh. After a while Bradfield stopped calling on me as often because my humorous sentences sometimes caused a little too much disruption.

When I first saw the poem *"Little Orphant Annie"* by James Whitcomb Riley in my seventh-grade English literature book, I asked Bradfield why a poem with so many grammatical errors was considered good enough to be in our literature book. She told me it was because the poet was able to capture the unique dialect of the people at the time. So that poem is an example of where correct English grammar didn't matter. Fortunately, Riley's poem, which was first published on November 15, 1885, is now in the public domain. That means I can share it here without breaking copyright laws, so here is the first poem I fell in love with:

LITTLE ORPHANT ANNIE

James Whitcomb Riley—1849-1916

Little Orphant Annie's come to our house to stay,
An' wash the cups an' saucers up, an' brush the crumbs
    away,

An' shoo the chickens off the porch, an' dust the hearth, an'
    sweep,
An' make the fire, an' bake the bread, an' earn her board-
    an'-keep;
An' all us other childern, when the supper things is done,
We set around the kitchen fire an' has the mostest fun
A-list'nin' to the witch-tales 'at Annie tells about,
An' the Gobble-uns 'at gits you
    Ef you
    Don't
    Watch
    Out!

Onc't they was a little boy wouldn't say his prayers,--
So when he went to bed at night, away up stairs,
His Mammy heerd him holler, an' his Daddy heerd him
    bawl,
An' when they turn't the kivvers down, he wasn't there at all!
An' they seeked him in the rafter-room, an' cubby-hole, an'
    press,
An' seeked him up the chimbly-flue, an' ever'wheres, I
    guess;
But all they ever found was thist his pants an' roundabout--
An' the Gobble-uns'll git you
    Ef you
    Don't
    Watch
    Out!

An' one time a little girl 'ud allus laugh an' grin,
    An' make fun of ever'one, an' all her blood an' kin;
An' onc't, when they was "company," an' ole folks was
    there,

She mocked 'em an' shocked 'em, an' said she didn't care!
An' thist as she kicked her heels, an' turn't to run an' hide,
They was two great big Black Things a-standin' by her side
,
An' they snatched her through the ceilin' 'fore she knowed
   what she's about!
An' the Gobble-uns'll git you
   Ef you
   Don't
   Watch
   Out!

An' little Orphant Annie says when the blaze is blue,
An' the lamp-wick sputters, an' the wind goes woo-oo!
An' you hear the crickets quit, an' the moon is gray,
An' the lightnin'-bugs in dew is all squenched away,--
You better mind yer parents, an' yer teachers fond an' dear,
An' churish them 'at loves you, an' dry the orphant's tear,
An' he'p the pore an' needy ones 'at clusters all about,
Er the Gobble-uns'll git you
   Ef you
   Don't
   Watch
   Out!

To this day, I can still recite this poem by memory. When I was in high school, I read it to my youngest sister, Jenny, and when I became a mother, I recited it by memory for my sons. My mother loved this poem, too, so every Halloween I'd call her up and recite it for her, too.

Bradfield also gave us poetry assignments to write limericks, which I loved writing because they came so easy for me.

Many of my classmates groaned when we got poetry assignments, and some of them wanted me to help them. I asked what they wanted their limerick to be about, such as a dog, cat, horse, duck, or rain. After the classmate chose the subject, I wrote the limerick. When Bradfield asked us to read our poems aloud, I read mine first, and the other students read the poems I wrote for them. Then Bradfield said, "Wow! We sure have a lot of talented poets in this class!" I snickered, but I wonder if she really knew I wrote them. I wish Bradfield would have lived long enough for me to thank her for making her English grammar classes so much fun.

My senior English teacher, Ordell (known as Lee) Paulson, also recognized me as a gifted writer. During my senior year, I volunteered to work on the school newspaper, and I always put a lot of effort into the assignments. One day in English class, Paulson brought a copy of the latest issue of the school paper to class, and he berated several students for the lack of effort they put into their stories. He said, "There were only two good stories in this entire paper ... and Barbara wrote both of them." Wow! Paulson complimented me in front of the entire class. That really made my day!

He also gave me an A+ on a short story I wrote titled "Professor Einstein and Planet Superior." I didn't keep a copy of that one, but I remember what it was about. Everyone on earth had to take a test every five years. Only those who scored high enough were allowed to remain on earth, so the powerful elite could carry out a plan to turn earth into "Planet Superior." Everyone else was put on spaceships and sent to other planets.

Paulson lived to be 89, and for several years I was included in his huge email list of friends. I'm grateful that I had the opportunity during those many communications to thank him for recognizing me for my writing skills.

Sergeant Major Gary G. Beylickjian also made a significant difference in my writing career. He served two tours, and he was wounded both in Korea and Vietnam. In 1971, he served as Chief of Army Newspapers. After his retirement, Beylickjian continued to have a major impact on the quality of Army newspapers. He read and edited hundreds of Army newspapers. During that time, I was editor of the *Northwest Guardian* newspaper at the former Fort Lewis Army post (now Joint Base Lewis McChord).

Beylickjian also personally made phone calls to spontaneously support and encourage Army editors, including me.

It would be difficult to express how grateful I was to receive that kind of feedback and words of encouragement. Beylickjian also produced several hundred issues of Post -30, a publication for Army newspapers. In fact, he published one of my poems—*"Writing with Passion"* in one of the Post -30 issues.

Every once in a while, Beylickjian awarded an Army journalist with the prestigious J-Award for outstanding journalism, and he gave me that award for a series of articles I wrote titled "Married to the Military." It meant the world to me to be recognized with that award from someone of his caliber.

Sadly, Beylickjian passed away on January 13, 2018, at age 86, and he was buried at Arlington National Cemetery. I wish he could have lived long enough for me to properly thank him for his awesome encouragement and support.

I recently saw a quote that read "Selfless giving is the art of living," and Beylickjian's legacy of continuing to help countless numbers of Army journalists after he retired (and without pay) showed that he had the "selfless giving" concept down to a T.

Barbara at age 75.

ABOUT THE AUTHOR

Confucius said, "Choose a job you love, and you will never have to work a day in your life."

Actually, Confucius was wrong. The more we love and enjoy our job, the more likely we are to work harder. Therefore, it would be more accurate to say, "Choose a career you love, and you will look forward to going to work every day."

Many people ask me why I chose to become a writer. Honestly, instead of me choosing it, I believe it chose me. Writing is something I've always loved and felt compelled to do—like breathing, eating, and sleeping. Writers have to write. It's almost like an addiction.

Most natural born writers also have an extraordinary ability to see and remember details of everything happening around them that most other people do not even notice. We might often be mistakenly labeled as daydreamers, when we are simply in deep thought, busy absorbing everything. Perhaps that's why I still have many vivid memories of people, places, and events as far back as age two.

Even when we know what we want to do for a living, it often takes many years to get there. Sadly, 50 years ago women were still being restricted from entering the field of journalism. The first time I applied for a job at a newspaper I was laughed at because women were not yet taken seriously as journalists. Many women who had journalism degrees were merely being used as glorified secretaries who were sometimes writing stories for their male counterparts but were not getting credit for them. So, I held many other jobs on my way to becoming a professional writer.

In some ways, that turned out to be a good thing because when I finally did become a newspaper reporter, I had a broad range of experiences that made it easier for me to write better stories. For example, when one of my beats was to write stories about childcare, I knew what kind of questions to ask during my interviews with child care managers because I had already owned and operated my own licensed childcare business called Harvey Rabbit's Day Care.

I supported my family for two years with that business when my first husband got out of the Navy to become a full-time ROTC student at the University of Washington.

Also, when I wrote stories about all of the difficulties spouses had to endure while their military husband or wife was deployed overseas, I knew firsthand what they were going through because I was a military spouse, too.

I was able to write stronger articles because I lived through some of the same experiences. That's why trainers often tell writers and speakers to write and speak about topics they know best. If we live it and feel it, we can make our readers or audience feel it, too. In fact, writing, speaking and reading pretty much go together. They are like first cousins. It's difficult to do one without the other.

Besides the Holy Bible, two books I read that had the greatest impact on my life for the better are *The Power of Positive Thinking* by Dr. Norman Vincent Peale and *Handbook to Higher Consciousness* by Ken Keyes.

They are both old books, but they are still very relevant today. I was only age 15 when I read Peale's book, and that's when I learned how important it is to develop a positive attitude and believe in ourselves. I was reading that book when I decided to sign up for a typing class in 10th grade. My two older sisters had already learned to type, and my next younger sister had just signed up for the typing class, too. For some reason my sisters teamed up against me and told Ma and Pa not to approve my choice of classes because I would never be able to learn how to type. Pa agreed and ordered me to take another class instead.

I felt devastated because having the skill to type was my ticket off the farm and into a good job in the Twin Cities. That's when my brother, the one I call Bernie, stood up and said, "If the other girls can learn how to type, Barbara can, too!"

Wow! I'll never forget that Bernie dared to defy Pa and stand up for me. When I saw Pa slap him down, I was all the more determined to take that typing class.

That's all it took—for one brother to believe in me—for me to believe in myself, too. It was my life, and I had a right to learn how to type so nothing would stop me. I signed Ma's signature of approval, but I still had to get the school counselor Doebbert's approval, too, and that was not easy. The first thing Doebbert did was look at my hands and say, "You should not take typing. You have short, stubby fingers, so you would fail the class."

I sure proved him wrong! I got straight As in the typing

class. I learned how to type faster than all of my doubting sisters, and I also won the "Best Typist of the Year" award in my senior year.

If I had not believed in myself against all odds, it would have prevented me from ever getting my dream job as a newspaper journalist. Now at age 75, I still type 100 words per minute, and that sure helps to write books, too.

Keyes' book covered how important it is to make the best of the things we can control in our lives and how to accept and cope with the things we cannot control. Keyes compared how white rats behaved in a maze to people in similar situations. His comparison made me laugh at the stupidity of some human behavior because the white rats appeared to be more intelligent.

By the time I graduated from high school, I had a shoe box under my bed full of poems. When I went home on a weekend to get them, I discovered my mother had thrown them in the trash because she thought they were just scraps of paper. One of my early poems was about teenage suicide. I don't remember the whole poem, but I repeated these words at the end of each stanza:

So, when you find that life is tough and much too hard to face

Please bring back your memory to this time and place,

And think about this poem I wrote with the words I said,

"Don't lie down all set to die before the day you're dead."

When I became a busy military spouse and mother, I stopped writing poetry for several years, but I never stopped writing. I typed letters on my old typewriter nearly every day. We did not yet have computers and could not yet communicate with email or Zoom. As an English-Writing (Journalism) major at the University of Puget Sound I took a poetry class, so I had to start writing more poems again. I thought it would be easy, but my poetry instructor only liked free verse. Before that, I thought poets who wrote free verse lacked the skill to know how to rhyme. Rhyming poetry comes easy for me, and it is a lot more difficult for me to write free verse. To do that, I have to work hard to take the rhyme out. Whenever I write a poem, the rhyme is usually automatically there. So that was a different experience for me.

Shortly after I graduated from the University of Puget Sound, I started working as a civil service employee at what used to be the Fort Lewis Army post (now Joint-Base Lewis/McChord). It took a while, but when a writing position became available at the *Northwest Guardian* Army newspaper in the public affairs office, I had all of the right credentials, and I got the job.

I loved working as a newspaper reporter because it was like getting paid to attend college. I learned something new every day. By having a press pass, I also got free front-row tickets to major public events and got to meet, interview, and photograph a wide variety of people who visited the post, including celebrities like Montel Williams and Chris Rock.

I am most proud that I never missed a deadline. Sometimes it meant I went without sleep and wrote all night long to get my story in on time. I understood the importance of meeting a deadline because editors could not put out a newspaper with a bunch of blank holes where a story was supposed to fill the space. Some of the most powerful stories I heard, however, never made it into the newspaper because we could never have printed them.

For example, every year I wrote stories during "Breast Cancer Awareness Week" in support of all women suffering from this dreaded disease. Now that so many years have passed, I will share a few examples with you because the people involved are most likely long gone. To protect everyone's privacy, I am not naming names.

One breast cancer survivor I interviewed had a double mastectomy. She said her doctors had plans to remove part of her buttocks to rebuild new breasts for her, which involved more surgery. In between her treatments, this courageous woman continued to work as many hours as she could because she needed the money to help pay for her medical bills that her insurance did not cover. What she told me next was a real shocker.

She had a very insensitive man for a boss. Actually, he was more than insensitive. He was a mean bully. This breast cancer survivor told me that for several days after she returned to work following her double mastectomy, her boss kept staring at her. One day he approached her desk and said, "Okay, I just have to ask you. What does it feel like to be a woman with no breasts?"

I said, "Oh, my goodness! What did you say?"

"I asked him if he really wanted to know and he said he did," she said.

So, this woman then told her boss to stand with his legs apart.

"Now grab hold of your balls, rip them off, go over there, and throw them out the window," she said. "That's what it feels like!"

I thought that was such an excellent response, and I asked her, "Then what did he say?"

"He just got a most horrible look on his face, said OUCH, and walked away. He never bothered me again," she said.

I also interviewed a gorgeous blonde woman with a knockout figure, who had to have her breasts removed because of breast cancer. I met her husband a few times, and I did not like him because he appeared to be rather self-centered and arrogant. Immediately after this woman's breast cancer surgery, her husband proved I was right about him because he walked out on his wife at a time when she needed him most. Any decent man who truly loves his wife will be even more supportive and devoted to his wife while she is undergoing treatment for this dreadful disease. This woman was heartbroken and begged her no-good husband to stay, but he just turned to her and said, "I'm sorry but I'm a man and what man wants to stay married to a boob-less woman?"

I assured her that she was better off not being married to a man like that. Furthermore, I told her that she was still young, pretty, and smart enough to find a better man who would love and appreciate her for all the right reasons. Sure enough, she soon had a much better man in her life.

Over the years, I interviewed many courageous women who fought and won their battle against various kinds of breast cancer. It's good to know more and more women are beating this dreaded disease.

God Bless all breast cancer survivors, and may God bless all decent men who stand by and support their wives throughout their treatments in their courageous fight to survive.

I retired from the Department of Defense in May 2009 at age 62. Since then, Army newspapers have been replaced with a military app. Soldiers can still get experience and train as broadcast journalists (MOS 46R) without a college degree, but that form of journalism is not for everyone. In fact, any form of journalism is not for anyone who does not have a true passion to write. Most journalism jobs are not Monday to Friday with weekends off because news happens 24-7. Therefore, journalists often miss family events or having fun weekends out with friends. Journalists who do not love to write will burn out in a hurry.

So far, my life has been an interesting journey. I feel blessed and grateful that I'm still waking up on this side of the ground.

CPSIA information can be obtained
at www.ICGtesting.com
Printed in the USA
BVHW030856210822
645035BV00007B/11